Teaching with Hip Hop in the 7–12 Grade Classroom

This book presents practical approaches for engaging with Hip Hop music and culture in the classroom. As the most popular form of music and youth culture today, Hip Hop is a powerful medium through which students can explore their identities and locate themselves in our social world. Designed for novice and veteran teachers, this book is filled with pedagogical tools, strategies, lesson plans, and real-world guidance on integrating Hip Hop into the curriculum. Through a wide range of approaches and insights, Lauren Leigh Kelly invites teachers to look to popular media culture to support students' development and critical engagement with texts.

Covering classroom practice, assessment strategies, and curricular and standards-based guidelines, the lessons in this book will bolster students' linguistic and critical thinking skills and help students to better understand and act upon the societal forces around them. The varied activities, assignments, and handouts are designed to inspire teachers and easily facilitate modification of the assignments to suit their own contexts.

The impact of Hip Hop on youth culture is undeniable; this is the perfect book for teachers who want to connect with their students, support meaning-making in the classroom, affirm the validity of youth culture, and foster an inclusive and engaging classroom environment.

Lauren Leigh Kelly is an Associate Professor of Urban Teacher Education at Rutgers University, USA.

T0386585

Other Eye on Education Books Available from Routledge

(www.routledge.com/eyeoneducation)

Teaching with Comics and Graphic Novels
Fun and Engaging Strategies to Improve Close Reading
and Critical Thinking in Every Classroom
Tim Smyth

Black Appetite. White Food.
Issues of Race, Voice, and Justice Within and
Beyond the Classroom
Jamila Lyiscott

Remote Teaching and Learning in the Middle and High ELA
Classroom Instructional Strategies and Best Practices
Sean Ruday and Jennifer Cassidy

Student-Centered Literacy Assessment in the 6–12 Classroom
An Asset-Based Approach
Sean Ruday and Katie Caprino

Culturally Relevant Teaching in the English Language Arts
Classroom A Guide for Teachers
Sean Ruday

What to Look for in Literacy
A Leader's Guide to High Quality Instruction
Angela Peery and Tracey Shiel

Identity Affirming Classrooms
Spaces that Center Humanity
Erica Buchanan-Rivera

From Texting to Teaching
Grammar Instruction in a Digital Age
Jeremy Hyler and Troy Hicks

Teaching with Hip Hop in the 7–12 Grade Classroom

A Guide to Supporting Students' Critical Development Through Popular Texts

Lauren Leigh Kelly, Ph.D.

Routledge
Taylor & Francis Group

NEW YORK AND LONDON

Cover image: [TBC]

First published 2024
by Routledge
605 Third Avenue, New York, NY 10158

and by Routledge
4 Park Square, Milton Park, Abingdon, Oxon, OX14 4RN

Routledge is an imprint of the Taylor & Francis Group, an informa business

Library of Congress Cataloging-in-Publication Data
Names: Kelly, Lauren Leigh, author.
Title: Teaching with hip hop in the 7–12 grade classroom : a guide to
   supporting students' critical development through popular texts /
   Lauren Leigh Kelly.
Description: New York, NY : Routledge, 2023. | Series: Eye on
   education | Includes bibliographical references.
Identifiers: LCCN 2022060331 | ISBN 9781032258010 (paperback) |
   ISBN 9781032276977 (hardback) | ISBN 9781003293767 (ebook)
Subjects: LCSH: English language—Study and teaching (Secondary) |
   Hip-hop. | Music in education. | Culturally relevant pedagogy.
Classification: LCC LB1631 .K438 2023 | DDC 428.0071/2—dc23/
   eng/20230331
LC record available at https://lccn.loc.gov/2022060331

ISBN: 978-1-032-27697-7 (hbk)
ISBN: 978-1-032-25801-0 (pbk)
ISBN: 978-1-003-29376-7 (ebk)

DOI: 10.4324/9781003293767

Typeset in Palatino
by Apex CoVantage, LLC

Access the Support Material: routledge.com/9781032258010

for my mothers,
Olivene, Carole, and Cherrie

Contents

Meet the Author

Lauren Leigh Kelly is an Assistant Professor of Urban Social Justice Teacher Education in the Graduate School of Education at Rutgers University. She is also the founder of the annual Hip Hop Youth Research and Activism Conference. An alum of Wesleyan University, St. John's University, and Teachers College, Columbia University, Kelly taught high school English for ten years in New York where she also developed courses in Hip Hop literature and culture, spoken word poetry, and theatre arts. Dr. Kelly's research focuses on adolescent critical literacy development, Black feminist theory, Hip Hop pedagogy, critical consciousness, and the development of critical, culturally sustaining pedagogies. Dr. Kelly's work has been nationally recognized, including receiving the Nasir Jones Fellowship at the Hutchins Center for African and African American Research at Harvard University, the National Academy of Education/Spencer Postdoctoral Research Fellowship; the Save the Kids Hip Hop Activism Scholar-Activist of the Year Award, the American Educational Research Association (AERA) Writing and Literacies Special Interest Group Steve Cahir Early Career Award, and the Rutgers GSE Alumni Association Distinguished Faculty Lecture Award.

Acknowledgments

As we know, teaching and learning for social justice is predicated on building, sustaining, and uplifting communities. My work inside and outside of the classroom, including the lessons shared in this book, are a direct result of the communities that have sustained and uplifted me through their love, patience, and generosity. I offer here my deepest gratitude to those named and unnamed who have taught me, learned with me, and dreamed with me.

Of course, neither I nor this book could exist without the love of my parents, Olivene Kelly and Tony Kelly, who have unceasingly encouraged my passion for teaching and learning.

This passion was also nurtured by my teachers who showed me how impactful schools can be in students' lives and futures, including Ellen Keuling, Gloria Miller, Denise Corazón, Alexis McGill (Johnson), Ashraf Rushdy, and Aracelis Girmay.

My teaching at the intersections of media, literacy, and social justice is also inspired by my brothers, Esteban Kelly and Brian Kelly, and the futures of their children, Skyler, Brayden, Anaïs, Gavin, and Saskia.

My curriculum and pedagogy have been co-created and revised with my students, especially those who were gracious and patient with me in my earliest days of teaching: Kazuki, Mika, Yukari, Mirai, Alex, Frone, Loany, Priscilla, Santiago, Ricky, Alasia, and countless others.

I also give thanks and appreciation to the following communities who have supported and guided me in my journey:

To my mentors who have carved out new paths and shown me how to create my own: Yolanda Sealey-Ruiz, Ernest Morrell, Christopher Emdin, Bettina Love, Leigh Patel, Cheryl McLean, Valerie Kinloch, Ariana Mangual-Figueroa, Scott Seider, Dave Stovall, Elaine "Docta E" Richardson, Bryonn Bain, Josef Sorett, Michelle Knight-Manuel.

To my sista-scholars who have consistently inspired and pushed my own thinking about how to hold and create spaces for BIPOC youth in schools and communities: Cati de los Ríos, Jamila Lyiscott, Limarys Caraballo, Sakeena Everett, Aaliyah El-Amin, Sherell McArthur, Tasha Austin, Kisha Porcher, Reshma Ramkellawan, Michelle Macchia, Lisa Knox-Brown, Crystal Belle, Keisha Green, Marcelle Mentor, Renata Love Jones, Grace Player, Billye Sankofa Waters, Bianca Nightengale-Lee, Christina "V" Villarreal, Bianca Baldridge.

To my Hip Hop education family: Aysha Upchurch, Justis Lopez, Vera Naputi, Mikal Amin Lee, Andrew "Dr. Ew" Carter, Crystal Leigh Endsley, Tony Keith Jr., Manny Faces, Mike Dando, Emery Petchauer, Ian Levy, Edmund Adjapong, Jason Rawls, John Robinson, Timothy Jones, Intikana, Stevie "Dr. View" Johnson, Dawn-Elissa "Dr. DEF" Fischer, Qiana Cutts, Justin Coles, Vajra Watson, Kyesha Jennings, Gabriel Ramirez, Tasha Iglesias.

To those who have created platforms for this family to teach and inspire others through Hip Hop Education: Martha Diaz, Michael Cirelli, Love Foy, Adam LeBow, Crystal Leigh Endsley, Aysha Upchurch, Walter Sistrunk, Ken Lindblom, Marcyliena Morgan.

To my partners and co-conspirators in teaching, leading, and life: Daren Graves, Nicole Mirra, Danielle Filipiak.

To my dear teacher friends working every day to build a better tomorrow with youth in K-12 classrooms: Jennifer Ievolo, Sarabeth Leitch, Brandi Kruse, Lamar Timmons-Long, Leila Estes, Stephen Holt, Tracy Ulmer, Mike Rush, Samantha Basile, Sonya Khanija.

To my friends and "Hip Hop Heads" who have constantly shown up for me and co-created spaces and ideas with me: Raven Maldonado, Vishrani Prag, Steven Toledo, Jen Byrd, Betsy Narvaez, Jerome "J-Roc" Joe, Adrian Silver, Danny Belinkie, and the "Queens" Crew: Anil Asokan, Joe Brenner, Sarah Gowrie, Phil Boda.

To the HHYRA youth who have taught me so much about love, pedagogy, and the power of intergenerational community-building: Safa, Sydney, Ally, Alondra, Darius, Naomi, Hector, Semaj, Keyke, Sanjana, Synciere, Niya.

To my current and former GSE students at Rutgers University who remind me why we do this work, including Brittany Marshall, Ajua Kouadio, Darnell Thompson, Tracy Petrosino, Rwan Elmohdli, Sam Marshall, Heather Harris, Lindsey Cortez, Dana Warhaftig, Brittany Egan, Alexander Lopez-Perez, Maya Smith-Mabry.

A special shout out to Sarabeth Leitch, Lamar Timmons-Long, and Jess Basile for reading and providing feedback on early drafts of this book.

To my editor, Karen Adler, who inspired the writing of the book and nurtured it with patience and empathy.

To the scholars who hold me accountable for creating and moving the words from my heart to the page: Caitlin Petre, Maya Pindyck, Laura Rigolosi, Earl O'Garro.

To Andre Charles, who encourages me every day to show up for and in community with youth.

And to all of my students, past, present, and future, who freedom dream for and with each other.

Support Material

Several of the Appendices and resources that appear in this book are also available on the Routledge website as downloadable files. Permission has been granted to purchasers of this book to download these tools and print them. You can access these downloads by visiting www.routledge.com/9781032258010. Then click on the tab that says "Support Material" and select the files. They will begin downloading to your computer.

Preface

In the first few weeks of my teaching career, I was teaching a summer school English class in a high school in Queens, NY, when one of my students, Alex, said to me, "I was listening to a rap song yesterday about school that you would hate. It's by a group called Dead Prez." "They schools?" I asked, "I love that song." I am not exaggerating when I tell you that Alex's jaw dropped. Incredulously, he said, "But you can't like that song. You're a teacher."

"They Schools," released in 2000 by the rap duo Dead Prez, is indeed one of my favorite songs. It offers a scathing critique of the American educational system by drawing connections between schools, prisons, and structural racism in society and by highlighting the impact of a Eurocentric curriculum on Black children's ability to learn and succeed in school. In fact, my own similar critiques of U.S. public schooling were the reason that I became a teacher in the first place. Therefore, Alex was not alone in his confusion.

From my perspective, Hip Hop, teaching, and anti-oppression went hand in hand. How dare I critique structures of oppression and not actively work to dismantle them? How could I have played "They Schools" on repeat for years and never considered what I could do to disrupt the harmful and dehumanizing practices enacted upon the most vulnerable youth in our schools? Of course I was in the classroom to challenge harmful schooling practices and not to reinforce them.

In my conversation with Alex about Dead Prez, a number of important things happened: The cultures, identities, and ideologies of this student overlapped with my own in ways that ruptured his understanding of teachers and teaching. This moment also revealed to me how many students view teachers— as willing participants of an oppressive educational system committed to upholding the status quo of schools. I realized that for Alex, my role as a teacher automatically put us at odds with one another, for I could not be both a public school educator *and* a Hip Hop Head—especially not the kind who aligns herself with the messages in Dead Prez's music. I also realized that if I was not transparent with my students about my identities—both as a Hip Hop head and as a critical educator, then how would they ever know that I was there as a co-conspirator (Love, 2019)? If I was to disrupt the longstanding structures of schooling that told Alex that teachers were inherently anti-Hip Hop and were not to be trusted, then I needed to bring my wholeness into the classroom and invite students to trust me with theirs. It was, therefore, this brief exchange with Alex in the first few weeks of my teaching career that birthed my teaching practice and my journey as a critical Hip Hop educator.

How to Use this Book

The purpose of this book is to share frameworks and strategies for working with Hip Hop texts and popular culture in the classroom. Chapter 1 provides background and context pertaining to the history and culture of Hip Hop and its role in students' critical and literacy development. Chapter 2 shares ideas for individual lessons and mini-units complete with instructions, examples, and song suggestions, along with a list of some of the ELA/ Literacy Common Core standards that one can find reflected in the lesson. Chapter 3 provides examples of assignments and assessments that are designed to be responsive to youth culture, the learning goals of a particular unit, and the values and sensibilities of Hip Hop. Chapter 4 shares guidelines for teachers who are developing or teaching a course on Hip Hop or popular culture. After these chapters, the *Appendices* provide additional resources for learning more about Hip Hop and Hip Hop education as well as for connecting with Hip Hop-based organizations.

This book contains examples of assignments, assessments, and handouts; however, these are not designed for teachers to simply photocopy and use as is. Rather, they are intended to be examples that can be remixed based on the social and cultural contexts of the students in the classroom. This remixing may involve adjusting the language, questions, or goals of the assignment; however, the resulting materials should still remain relevant for students and attentive to the values and history of Hip Hop culture. Similarly, the lessons shared throughout this book are meant to be guides for teachers in developing classroom activities that support the academic and socio-emotional development of the students based on who they are and how they are already engaging with the world.

Readers should also consider that the stories and examples provided in this book draw from my own experiences as a high school English language arts teacher in the northeastern United

States. Teachers of other subject areas and in other geographic regions may need to further adapt lessons to meet the grade level, subject area, and geographic context of their classrooms. This consideration also applies to the song suggestions throughout this book. I present these texts as powerful works of Hip Hop literature with the awareness that they are also reflective of my own cultural values and northeastern upbringing. Thus, these songs serve best as *examples* of the types of texts that the lessons make use of, and teachers should look to these suggestions for inspiration rather than as universally relatable content.

Relatedly, readers should also be mindful that as popular media culture shifts and grows, so do our individual and collective perspectives on popular media and those who create it. As a result of increasing public access to information and to the inner lives and identities of public figures, we are able to quickly learn new information about celebrities, including Hip Hop artists, which may impact how we view their music and their standing in popular media culture. Thus, teachers less informed about popular media culture should consider doing research on suggested artists before introducing them into the classroom. This research might result in a decision to avoid particular artists in the curriculum, or perhaps teachers might facilitate dialogue with students about how or if one distinguishes between the art and the artist.

In order to choose popular texts that are meaningful and culturally relevant for their students, teachers should seek input from current and/or former students regarding the songs and artists that are popular amongst youth in that particular area and age group. Once teachers have a list of some of the music that youth in the area are engaging with, they can start to plug these songs and artists into music streaming sites whose algorithms will automatically suggest related music. This gives teachers a wealth of songs to choose from as well as autonomy in selecting the texts to be studied in the classroom. It is vital to note that teachers who consider themselves Hip Hop Heads or tuned in to popular culture should also be gathering suggestions from students since our positionality as non-youth will always make us outsiders to and, ideally, students of youth culture.

In fact, one of the biggest challenges of teaching with popular texts is that popular culture, particularly youth culture, is constantly shifting and, therefore, cannot be canonized or "mastered." Therefore, I encourage educators to work towards mastery over their *approaches* to working with popular texts in the classroom, rather than over youth culture or popular texts. In order for teachers to truly center their students' experiential wisdom, I also encourage teachers to develop a comfort in not knowing and in listening to and learning from students.

1

Introduction

One day, while walking through the hallway of the high school in which I was teaching, I overheard two Black girls reciting lyrics to a Kendrick Lamar song entitled "Backseat Freestyle," the third track on Lamar's 2012 album *good kid, m.A.A.d. city*, as they strolled towards class. In unison, they recited Lamar's lyrics announcing that he has many "bitches," including his "wifey, girlfriend, and mistress" (Lamar, 2012), counting off the latter three assets by holding up a finger in the air for each. As an outspoken critical educator, I could not help but react. "Ladies," I said, "should we talk about this?" The girls gave me a knowing glance, giggled, and continued on to class.

In an interview with Hot 97's Cipha Sounds, Peter Rosenberg, and K Foxx, Kendrick Lamar explained that this song, as well as the album itself, was about "being in the mind state of being six-teen years old, and not having no cares in the world. Not giving a damn about nothing, but life and money and what you see in front of you . . . and being under the influence of everything" (Hot 97 NY, 2012). Based on Lamar's description of the song and album, it makes sense that its lyrics would appeal to youth, especially those maintaining similar attitudes about life. I later discussed the song lyrics with a former student of mine, Jake, who echoed Lamar's explanation that the song is a reflection of his attitude as a younger version of himself before he matured into the thoughtful, self-reflective artist he is widely known as; therefore, Jake said, the song should be taken as a criticism of

DOI: 10.4324/9781003293767-1

the very attitude it projects. I wondered if the girls that I had encountered that day in the hallway had this same interpretation of the song. If so, reciting these lyrics in which women are referred to in a manner that could be viewed as disposable or dehumanizing is certainly an interesting choice with complex implications.

Months after the hallway moment described earlier, I was in my classroom preparing to teach my 10th grade English class when Meghan, a white female student in my class, absent-mindedly strolled into the room reciting the beginning of 2 Chainz's first verse on his song "Birthday Song," which describes someone who has a "big booty," so he calls her "Big Booty" (Epps & West, 2012). Knowing Meghan, I was aware that she was simply repeating the lyrics to a popular song and did not intend to enact or portray an ideological stance in doing so. At the same time, I couldn't help but wonder what it meant for this student, who is not an insider of the culture that created this song and did not in any way resemble the women portrayed in the song's video, to be engaging in the consumption of this music and repeating lyrics that ostensibly can be viewed as dehumanizing and misogynistic towards Black women. Somehow, this felt related to but different from the Black girls in the hallway reciting Kendrick Lamar's lyrics.

The latter example also recalls for me a moment that occurred once between Lisa, a Black female student, and Christa, a white female student, in my 12th grade English class one year. The two students had stayed after class to watch a newly released Nicki Minaj video that had received criticism in the media. After watching the first part of the video, both girls shook their heads and expressed their disappointment in Minaj. Then Lisa pointed out the difference in how the two girls were processing this media text, telling Christa, "You don't have to claim her. Well, as a female, you do but not as a Black person" (Kelly, 2016). In this brief moment between classes, Lisa stumbled upon the profound understanding that whether or not she approved of the music created by particular Black female artists, she felt innately tied to them due to her own identity as a Black girl. On the other hand, although Christa was also a girl, she was not Black and, therefore, popular imagery or messages depicting Black girlhood or womanhood did not impact her in the same way. Perhaps Lisa's understanding helps to shed light on why Meghan's "Birthday Song" recitation struck me as being fraught with complexities regarding race, gender, sexuality, and representation in popular music. I knew that I didn't have answers to the questions that these moments brought up for me, but I certainly wanted to explore them with the very population most impacted by the ubiquity of Hip Hop music and culture.

Understanding Hip Hop Culture

The history of Hip Hop is intricate and vast and warrants a thorough study in order for one to fully grasp the paradoxical inevitability and impossibility of its existence. Readers should visit *Appendices A* and *B* for a list of texts that provide a more comprehensive understanding of Hip Hop and its history than I can distill here. For the purpose of engaging with this book, however, it is essential to know that Hip Hop culture originated from Black and Latinx youth in New York City and consists of five elements: DJing, emceeing/rapping, graffiti writing, breaking (b-boying/b-girling), and knowledge, also referred to as "Knowledge of Self." The latter element is often seen as the most central to Hip Hop culture since participation in Hip Hop's artistic mediums is a form of self-exploration and expression as well as a means to know and engage with others. All four artistic elements work together to construct Hip Hop culture and community and can be traced back to forms of Black ancestral practice (Love, 2016).

Djing, at its most basic level, is the practice of "spinning" records, or tracks simultaneously or in succession such that there is no space in between. DJ Kool Herc is credited with birthing Hip Hop since, after moving as an adolescent from Jamaica, W.I. to the Bronx, NY, he began playing music at parties in the Bronx and was the first to use two turntables at once to continuously play the breakbeats of funk and disco songs, allowing for the breakers to dance uninterrupted at the party, rather than waiting for the breaks in each song to come on. The breakbeat, thus, became the sound of Hip Hop, with emcees spitting rhymes, or rapping, over these beats. Although early raps began as a way to "hype up" or move the crowd at parties, with the DJ still being the focal point of the entertainment, these rhymes became increasingly more intricate and eventually became as inextricable from Hip Hop music as the DJ.

Of course, Hip Hop music would not exist without the b-boys and b-girls who recognized early on that the breakbeat provided an ideal sound by which to breakdance, an innovative style of movement developed by Black and Latinx youth in New York City and which consists of toprocking, downrocking, power moves, and freezes. At these same parties, as well as across New York City, Black and Latinx youth were also developing a new style of art, graffiti writing. Graffiti art encompasses written words, or "tags" as well as images, with many graffiti pieces containing a combination of these, all of which make use of uniquely stylized fonts and forms and which are typically painted on walls and public structures, such as train cars.

In its earlier years, Hip Hop represented a means of seeking joy and escape for urban youth who were experiencing the lasting impacts of structural and racial oppression in the form of poverty, displacement, unemployment, drug addiction, and violence (Chang, 2005). Within this context, Hip Hop emerged as a clear example of the creativity and resilience of youth of color. In spite of this and of the fact that Hip Hop is now often celebrated as a popular form of art and culture, it is important to recognize that Hip Hop culture has been historically demonized. One example of this is in the case of graffiti writer Michael Stewart who, one night in 1983, was arrested and beaten by eleven transit police for tagging a subway platform and died less than two weeks later from his injuries (Chang, 2005). In the early '90s, there were campaigns led by influential groups and figures, including Dolores Tucker and then-second lady Tipper Gore, to censor and vilify rap music, claiming that its content was violent, sexually explicit, and a danger to youth (Chang, 2005). In 1993, Reverend Calvin Butts organized an "anti-rap rally" on Adam Clayton Powell Jr. Boulevard in Harlem and demonstratively steamrolled a pile of cassette tapes and CDs that he and his supporters considered offensive. More recently, in 2012, Jordan Davis, a Black, 17-year-old high school student was shot and killed by Michael Dunn, a white man, after Davis refused to turn down the rap music playing in his car. Even in schools, symbols of Hip Hop culture or urban culture are often criminalized through dress code policies that forbid hooded sweatshirts, sneakers, or baggy pants.

Importantly, it is not all followers of rap music and Hip Hop who are castigated for their consumption or participation in the culture, but specifically "We who are dark" (Love, 2019, p. 1). In fact, the criminalization of Hip Hop as well as that of Black and Brown youth and communities is as much a part of Hip Hop's history and resonance as is its artistry. Thus, as my student Lisa pointed out, the ability to consume Hip Hop culture without being subject to the oppression faced by those who created and are represented by it is a luxury as well as an indicator that the structures of oppression that Hip Hop was created to disrupt are still in place.

The Case for Critical Hip Hop Literacies in Secondary Education

As evidenced in the opening examples, popular media texts are complex, embedded with ideological values, and widely disseminated across mass audiences of consumers who may or may not be mindful of their participation in the perpetuation of the ideas that they are receiving through such texts. While the majority of America's youth are engaged in popular cultural practices through music, videos, and various digital media (Hobbs, 2020), few students have a safe, consistent, and critical space in which to reflect on and discuss the messages that dominate this media. As a result, young people whose identities and worldviews are influenced by popular media often construct identities that are limited, marginalizing, and potentially self-destructive. The danger in this is not simply that consumers receive ideas based on popular media but rather that few alternatives exist when it comes to popular media representations (Kellner & Share, 2007; Rose, 2003). This is especially so for consumers of mainstream Hip Hop music since commercial Hip Hop—that which is most popular and easily available to the public—contains particularly narrow and limited representations of urban communities and communities of color (Rose, 2008). Without the space to examine these representations and construct new ones, young consumers of popular culture run the risk of emulating the very identity representations that exploit and limit them (Kellner & Share, 2005).

In a society consumed by ever-increasing media and digital technology, it is paramount that schools provide their students with the skills and tools necessary to analyze, interpret, deconstruct, and construct media images and messages. As Alim (2011) noted, "school culture has been eclipsed in kids' lives by media culture" (pp. 238–239). Consequently, it is the role of educators to engage with popular media in the classroom, not simply for the sake of student engagement but for the purpose of supporting students in developing meaningful literacy practices. Thus, it is through the practice of critical literacy, the act of "questioning received knowledge and immediate experience with the goal of challenging inequality and developing an activist citizenry" (Shor, 1999, p. 8), that educators can provide students with the space and tools for meaningful engagement with and reflection upon the multiple texts that surround them. As an approach to the reading and writing of texts, critical literacies invite students to become critical thinkers by engaging in the process of decoding the language and ideas embedded in texts in order to analyze their meanings as well as their implications for themselves and for society. Critical media literacies build on this practice by including media texts as a site of analysis in critical literacy instruction, encouraging students to become critical consumers and creators of digital texts and popular culture.

Critical Hip Hop literacy, then, as explored in this book, is an approach to the study of popular culture that allows for the ideologies, representations, and tensions present in society and reflected in Hip Hop culture to be addressed. It validates Hip Hop as a literary and cultural form, while also providing a space to be reflective about its content and proactive in resisting, responding to, and creating its messaging. Engaging with critical Hip Hop literacies in school also supports students' development of critical consciousness, or their ability to analyze, navigate, challenge, and transform structures of oppression and inequity in society (Seider et al., 2021). To this end, this book is designed to support secondary-level humanities teachers in utilizing popular texts in the classroom for discussion and reflection that can foster students' critical, literacy, sociopolitical, and identity development. Using critical Hip Hop literacy as a framework, the following chapters support teachers' development of classroom lessons and curriculum that best meet the specific needs of the spaces in which they teach and the students whom they teach.

Glossary of Terms

Black: refers to those who identify as part of the African diaspora, including those residing within or outside of the United States and those who are descendants of Africans previously enslaved in the U.S.

critical consciousness: one's ability to recognize, analyze, and challenge structures of oppression.

critical literacies: approaches to the reading and creation of texts that analyzes and challenges relationships of power and inequity.

critical media literacies: approaches to the reading and creation of media that analyze and challenge relationships of power and inequity.

critical Hip Hop literacies: approaches to the reading and creation of Hip Hop texts and culture that analyze and challenge relationships of power and inequity.

culturally relevant pedagogy: a framework developed by Dr. Gloria Ladson-Billings (1995) which honors the cultures and identities of minoritized students and positions these as assets integral to their academic success and critical consciousness development.

Hip Hop head: a person who is a lifelong enthusiast of Hip Hop music or culture.

Hip Hop music: a genre of music that includes rap, R&B, and reggae crossovers.

Hip Hop culture: encompasses the five elements of DJing, emceeing, breaking, graffiti writing, and developing knowledge of self and also includes language, fashion, dance, and values often reflected in Hip Hop music.

Hip Hop pedagogy: teaching with or about Hip Hop in a way that authentically engages with Hip Hop cultural values and practices.

Hip Hop text: any artifact of or related to Hip Hop culture that can be "read," including lyrics, articles, narratives, videos, etc.

minoritized, marginalized: underrepresented, misrepresented, underserved, and disempowered as well as made to feel peripheral, invisible, or insignificant in schools and in society.

popular media engagement: interaction with popular culture through listening to music, watching videos, watching television, and reading materials (i.e., magazine articles or blogs).

Positionality: refers to the impact of one's multiple identities and sociopolitical locations on their perspective and interactions with their social environment, including their experiences of power, dominance, or marginalization.

sampling: the practice of taking parts of existing songs or artifacts and repurposing them to make something new.

sociopolitical: of or relating to the multitude of social and political factors impacting society, including manifestations of race, class, gender, and power inequities.

A Note on Honoring the Full Humanity of Students

As stated earlier, Hip Hop music and culture are embedded with complex representations regarding power, especially as it pertains to race, class, gender, and sexuality. For this reason, the study of Hip Hop offers an ideal site for constructing, interrogating, and challenging harmful ideologies. Simultaneously, teaching with Hip Hop can exacerbate the harm that minoritized students already face in schools if done myopically. In order to avoid this, I offer the following considerations for teachers working with Hip Hop texts in classrooms.

A misconception that teachers sometimes have about youth of color is that they are all participants in rap music and culture. As many of my students, including Lisa, have revealed to me, youth of color may feel inherently *tied* to Hip Hop artistry; however, this does not mean that they are active consumers or participants in the music or culture. Assuming students' Hip Hop identities based on their racial identities can limit students' freedom to be and show up as their full selves in the classroom. Hill's (2009) discussion of the tensions between Blackness and authenticity that arose while he was teaching a high school Hip Hop Literature class highlights the danger of conflating Blackness with Hip Hop identity.

> "For some of the Black students, failure to satisfy the conditions of authentic Blackness made them feel unauthorized to fully participate in certain aspects of classroom life. For example . . . on a note attached to her final assignment, [Michelle] offered the following explanation for her lack of participation: "It's not that I don't like the class. It's just that I grew up different, so I don't know a lot of the stuff that they talk about. . . . I'm not really hip-hop so I don't talk as much as I do in normal classes."
>
> (p. 63)

For Hill's student, Michelle, the combination of her being Black and not having a Hip Hop identity led to her feeling like an outsider in class, resulting in her withdrawal from class discussion. In my own teaching experiences, I have spoken to several Black students who felt similarly "othered" in school due to their participation in popular cultural practices that were not Hip Hop, leading to other students questioning their Black authenticity. In fact, I have even heard teachers refer to certain Black students as "not really Black" based on the linguistic and cultural practices that they displayed. In order to avoid essentializing or further marginalizing youth, teachers must be mindful not to make assumptions about their students based on their race, ethnicity, language, or geographic positioning.

In addition to avoiding stereotypes, teachers should also be careful not to be extractive of students by relying on them to perform the labor of teaching the class or their teachers about their identities. Oftentimes as educators, we expect students to be prepared to teach about the cultures that they participate in when these cultures are different from our own. The assumption here is that students are willing to teach and that they are prepared to do so. This puts a great deal of onus on students who may not have volunteered to serve as teachers or ambassadors of their culture. It is also not the responsibility of students to fill in gaps in students' or educators' knowledge. Therefore, before asking students to share their expertise, teachers should ensure that students are truly willing to spend their time and energy in this way and that they have the appropriate resources to do so.

Even when students do volunteer to share their expertise in class, teachers should be sure not to allow students' singular narratives to stand in for an entire culture or community. I have seen this occur in my graduate courses when there is one student who has an experience different from the majority and is, thus, leaned upon by the other students to share their knowledge. Although the student's experiences should not be called into question, teachers can contextualize their contributions with additional sources and information such that students' individual narratives are not assumed to be representative of all who share their identities.

A final note of caution is for teachers to be mindful of how their own positionality as well as that of the students might impact students' reception of particular language, imagery, or themes that are reflected in class texts. More specifically, uncurated media exposure can run the risk of exacerbating, rather than challenging, existing biases and stereotypes of minoritized communities. It is for this reason that the suggested texts in this book should not be used blindly but should be considered within the context of who is in the room and what conversations are healthy for them to have or to witness. (For example, engaging in a discussion of the use of the "n" word in rap music could be very enlightening and fruitful for Black American students. However, this is not a conversation for white students or teachers, and their participation in such a dialogue could cause harm to the Black students in the room.) In what follows, I share additional examples of the need to select texts in ways that protect marginalized and vulnerable students in the classroom.

In a one-day teacher workshop that I facilitated, I asked participants to work in groups to analyze and create an interpretive performance of a popular song by selecting one of several sets of lyrics that I brought for the workshop. One of the songs available was the reggae song "Ghetto Story, Chapter 2" by Baby Cham featuring Alicia Keys. This song, which contains verses in Jamaican patois, tells an uplifting tale of surviving a difficult living environment to eventually find success and the ability to give back to one's community. I decided to include this song as an example of how teachers can acknowledge Jamaican patois as a linguistic practice that is often invisiblized in schools and center the identities of West Indian students in their classrooms. I also made sure that there was a surplus of song options so that this song would only be selected by participants who had Jamaican patois as part of their linguistic repertoire. Unfortunately, during the workshop, I forgot to clarify this instruction before the groups got up to choose their songs from the table.

Realizing this, I quickly went to find the group that had selected "Ghetto Story, Chapter 2," and when I discovered that no one from the group had a background in Jamaican patois, I suggested that they avoid using any exact lyrics for those verses and instead translate or summarize the context of those lines. I also offered to help with the translation since I do have Jamaican heritage and familiarity with the language. The group members said that they were okay at the moment and would let me know if they needed anything. I trusted that the group knew how to work with the text and went to check on other groups. However, when the group began to perform, I discovered that they had decided to have one of the group members, a white woman who was not a speaker of Jamaican patois, read Baby Cham's exact lyrics aloud in a performance that inadvertently came across as a mockery, rather than a celebration, of Jamaican patois. The issue here is not with the text itself or with the racial identity of the woman who recited Baby Cham's verses but rather that the text that the group selected was not linguistically appropriate for its members. Due to the group members' positionalities, their performance of this reggae song was received by the audience as inauthentic at best, and disrespectful to some.

In addition to attending to language content, teachers should also consider if the texts they are selecting are developmentally, culturally, and *contextually* appropriate for students. One year, while teaching a 12th-grade writing class, I facilitated a class viewing of Byron Hurt's (2006) film, *Hip Hop: Beyond Beats and Rhymes*, a powerful documentary that examines misogyny, homophobia, and hypermasculinity in rap music and culture. Having watched this film a number of times, including in previous high school classrooms with students, I was excited to engage this class in discussions about this film. What I did not consider was that this particular class was racially diverse, unlike the predominantly Black and Latinx classes that I had taught previously. Thus, it did not occur to me that the racial dynamics of this class would impact the students' reception of the documentary.

However, on the first day that I showed the film in class, a few of the Black students stayed after to express their hurt, anger, and frustration at me. At first, I did not understand, thinking perhaps the students disagreed with the film's criticism of rap culture. This was not the case. Rather, the students did not appreciate my "airing the dirty laundry" of the Black community with white students in the room. They felt exposed and, worse, that the criticism was unbalanced. "Are we gonna watch a film about the bad stuff that white people do?" They asked.

Similar to Hill's (2009) description of his Hip Hop Literature class, I had not equated the study of rap music and culture with the study of Blackness, but my Black students did. And for them, if there was going to be any study of Blackness within this racially diverse context, it must shed a positive light on their race rather than a critical one.

Once again, it was not the text itself but the context in which it was shown, specifically the racial dynamics of the class, that led to the film being an inappropriate choice for this classroom since it further othered students who were already experiencing marginalization as Black students in a racially diverse school. Additionally, my students expected me, their Black teacher, to know better. Thus, the positionality of students and teachers must be considered when working with particular texts, language, or themes in the classroom. This does not mean that teachers should avoid working with explicit or meaty content; rather, when this content is brought into classroom lessons, it should be done thoughtfully and in such a way that any harmful stereotypes, ideologies, or misconceptions reflected in the texts are the subject of classroom interrogation rather than propagation.

Language and Censorship in Hip Hop Education

A question that I often hear from students and educators is regarding how I address explicit language when working with popular media in the classroom. There are multiple strategies that teachers can employ for dealing with mature content in classroom texts, and there is certainly no right answer to this question except that teachers remain thoughtful and consistent in their approach.

In thinking about how to address explicit content in classroom teaching, it is necessary to consider that this content already exists in young people's lives outside of the classroom. The majority of America's youth already engages with multiple forms of media through devices such as computers, smartphones, and tablets. Although some of this content can be limited through mechanisms such as parental controls and firewalls, most secondary educators are well aware that students consistently find ways around these controls and share these methods with each other. Thus, young people are exposed to explicit content regardless of what we do in the classroom. If students are already accessing mature content through their media consumption outside of school, then it becomes the responsibility of teachers to provide students with an environment for engaging in healthy dialogue about this content as well as strategies for reading and thinking critically about how media texts impact their lives outside of the classroom.

When considering whether or not to include popular texts with explicit language in classroom teaching, teachers should consider the guidelines stated previously regarding texts that are culturally, contextually, and developmentally appropriate based on what they know of their students. Additionally, teachers can establish guidelines with their students for reading texts that contain explicit language. I witnessed a clear example of this one day during an observation of a high school English class that was reading the play *Topdog/Underdog* by Suzan-Lori Parks, a profound dramatic work that explores the legacies of history, slavery, and familial trauma through the narratives of two young men who are brothers. The dialogue in this text is replete with explicit words and mature content. As an observer watching the students engage in a read-aloud of this work, I was initially caught off guard by hearing some of the explicit language coming from the students' mouths. I was even more surprised by the absence of reaction from the students. There was no giggling, snickering, or furtive exchanges between students. In essence, the students dealt with this mature content maturely and subsequently engaged in meaningful literary dialogue about the themes of the text. Working with popular media in the classroom is no different from this example. It simply requires a mutual trust that students can handle this material with maturity and that teachers will facilitate an earnest and engaging study of the text.

Even with the aforementioned arguments for working with explicit language in classroom instruction, there are situations in which teachers may need to use edited or "clean" versions of song lyrics in their teaching. There are multiple ways to go about doing this. First, search for the song lyrics on the internet.[1] Copy and paste the song lyrics into a document, making sure to remove any hyperlinks as these can cause formatting issues. Some songs may already have a "clean" version, sometimes referred to as a "radio edit." If you do find this version, be sure to look it over before printing or sharing it with students since this pre-edited version might still have content that you do not find appropriate for your class. If "clean" lyrics are not available, then you can manually edit the text by replacing the words in question with either a blank space to indicate that something has been removed or with an alternate word in brackets that retains the same meaning but is more appropriate for your classroom. (The brackets are important for maintaining transparency with students that these are not the original words of the artist.)

A more advanced version of this process involves using alternate words that also retain the same rhyme quality or rhythmic effect as the original word. (For example, replacing the word, "Bitch" with "chick," since they both have a similarly derogatory connotation, depending on the context, and share an aural quality through the consistent "I" sound and consonance at the end of the word.) When finished editing, teachers may want to double-check the lyrics for explicit language by using the "search" or "find" tool to ensure that any words determined to be inappropriate have been removed.

Once, when I explained this editing process to teachers in a workshop, one participant raised the concern that editing song lyrics for the classroom was a form of censorship and that she disapproved of this practice. In response to this concern, I will state here that in no way is the editing of song lyrics a mandatory practice of Hip Hop pedagogy. Ultimately, the question of whether or not one should edit lyrics, as well as how the process of editing might impact the artwork, is one that teachers should take up with themselves and, perhaps, with their students. It is, however, worth noting that editing content for adolescent education is much the same as editing a song to be played on the radio or a movie to be played on television, both of which are common occurrences. The goal in these scenarios is to ensure that the media text has wider exposure and that those for whom particular portions of the text may be too mature are still able to access it in a developmentally appropriate format.

An additional option for addressing language in popular texts for the classroom is to have students participate in the process of editing. As discussed previously, students are likely to have already heard much of the language that is deemed inappropriate for the classroom. In fact, many students will have already memorized all of the lyrics to some of these songs. A powerful exercise for students, then, is to participate in the process of editing song lyrics before they are studied in class. This could perhaps happen as a whole-class activity to engage in a meaningful discussion with students about the politics of language and respectability or as an individual assignment in which students work on their own to edit song lyrics before bringing them into class or before sending them to the teacher to print for the class. In this way, students are asked to critically engage with the complexities of language in popular media and the implications of their language use for creating an equitable and loving classroom environment.

Note

1   The website Genius.com is often a great source for accurate song lyrics due to its crowdsourcing format.

2

Hip Hop Pedagogies in Classroom Practice

Oftentimes, teachers eager to bring Hip Hop education into their classrooms grapple with the apparent contradiction between teaching for academic achievement and teaching for social justice, as though we must choose one over the other. Yet, Emdin (2016) reminds us that successful teaching of any sort "focuses on making the local experiences of the student visible and . . . [positioning] the student as the expert in his or her own teaching and learning" (p. 27). Hip Hop as cultural and literary text offers educators the opportunity to do just that. The following lessons provide teachers with structures for the development of Hip Hop-based curriculum and pedagogy that bridges the gap between classroom learning and students' cultural and literacy practices, centering students' identities while equipping them with the skills they will need to navigate and transform their academic, social, and cultural communities.

Lessons One and Two

Building Hip Hop Classroom Community
For teachers to authentically engage with Hip Hop and popular culture in the classroom, it is imperative that this engagement occurs across all aspects of the classroom, including in

DOI: 10.4324/9781003293767-2

the building of the classroom community and culture. In what follows, I describe two examples of "icebreaker" or opening activities that teachers can implement during the initial days of a new class in order to establish the classroom as a space that invites students' identities and cultures and one that engages explicitly with youth cultures and popular media.

"Find Someone Who"

This activity is a take on the traditional "Find Someone Who" exercise (often called "Find Someone Who Bingo"), which typically encourages dialogue and connection amongst students by providing prompts for them to seek out others in the classroom based on specific descriptors. Some classic examples are, "Find someone who lives in the same neighborhood as you," or "Find someone who plays a musical instrument." The handout for this exercise often looks like a Bingo board, with a large square divided into multiple boxes with a different prompt in each box. As students find a person who can attest to one of the statements on the page, they obtain that person's name or signature and continue until they have completed a row or filled out all of the boxes. Through this exercise, students are encouraged to interact with one another and learn things about their peers that they otherwise may not have discovered. However, traditional approaches to this activity, while useful, are typically devoid of particular attention to the complex identities of young people and are a missed opportunity to foster more profound connections among students.

This Hip Hop-based approach to "Find Someone Who" embeds Hip Hop culture and practices in the development of prompts for the activity. Rather than focusing on broad categories of identity, such as having a talent or living near another student, the Hip Hop-based prompts are designed to reflect engagement with youth popular culture and foster students' connections through youth culture. These prompts can also signal to students that their cultures and identities are welcome in the classroom and that their teacher has expressed a commitment to learning about and engaging with youth culture. Some examples of Hip Hop-based approaches to this activity include the following: 1) Find someone who can name the five elements of Hip Hop culture;

2) Find someone who can perform a TikTok dance; 3) Find someone who can finish the line, "It was all a dream"; 4) Find someone who can name ten rappers who are women; 5) Find someone who can freestyle. (Note that the term "freestyle" in Hip Hop can refer to unscripted or unchoreographed rapping, dancing, or graffiti.)

Notice that in contrast to traditional approaches to this activity, the Hip Hop-based approach has an added performative element. It is not sufficient for a student to simply say that they can freestyle or name ten rappers who are women; rather, they must, as we say in Hip Hop culture, "show and prove" this knowledge or skill. Prompts such as the aforementioned examples have the potential to foster classroom community in the following ways: 1) Establishing the classroom as a space in which students can be vulnerable, celebrated, and supported (e.g., by having students freestyle, dance, etc.); 2) Centering youth knowledge and honoring students' knowledge of popular culture and Hip Hop culture in the classroom; 3) Engaging in collective learning and youth teaching; 4) Celebrating students' identities and multiple forms of knowing, being, and doing. Perhaps most significantly, this activity can resist the marginalization of students from non-dominant communities by highlighting forms of knowledge and practice that are typically absent or denigrated in school spaces. Additionally, the development of prompts for this activity encourages educators to remain tuned in to the ever-shifting landscape of youth popular culture by requiring teachers to update the prompts so as to remain relevant and to engage with current or former students by inviting them to contribute ideas for prompts.

I initially developed the Hip Hop-based "Find Someone Who" activity as an icebreaker for a youth conference that I facilitated with adolescents from a diversity of school settings who were meeting each other for the first time. As the first activity of the day, this warm-up ultimately shaped and grounded youth participation in the conference. In this particular instance, the process of the students collecting names for the worksheets was instrumental in breaking through the tensions of meeting new people and developing comfort in the space; however, it was during the "show and prove" stage that the youth community of the conference was forged. During this portion of the activity, the knowledge, skills, and identities of the students flourished. These young people who had just met moments before expressed trust and vulnerability with one another, genuinely engaging in this collective learning experience while rhyming, dancing, teaching, and cheering each other on. Hip Hop has the tendency to do this: break down barriers and façades in communal spaces since it is built on the values of community and self-knowledge.

One distinct moment that I recall of facilitating this activity at the youth conference is when two students performed a dance simultaneously during the "show and prove" phase as though they were partners who had rehearsed this before even though they met for the first time that day. There is an instantaneous community that can be formed through engagement with Hip Hop culture in educational spaces. This activity also had an intergenerational element, as some of the teachers present were able to share knowledge and skills that their students had not seen. Thus, the Hip Hop-based "Find Someone Who" is more than simply an ice-breaker or warm-up activity; it is an opportunity for community-building, self-expression, and an authentic celebration of youth and Hip Hop culture.

Suggested Timeline
20–40 minutes or 1 Class Period at the beginning of the semester or unit

Materials

♦ Printed out or downloadable/copiable document of sheet with prompts and directions
♦ Optional: Instrumental music for potential freestyle
♦ Optional: Prize for the winner(s) if you choose to make this a competitive activity

Activity Directions for Teachers
Preparation: Prepare a handout with approximately 8–10 prompts and directions. You can design this in the Bingo card style or as a list (See sample that follows). Consider collaborating with current or former students for prompt suggestions based on current popular cultural references and practices.

Facilitation: Explain to students that this is a warm-up activity that requires communicating with others and getting to know classmates. Determine if students are playing competitively (i.e., as a game that someone can win or casually with no winners). Students should not sign their name to a prompt that they are unable or unwilling to "show and prove." Depending on how many students are present, determine the limit on how many times a single student can sign their name on one handout. (For example, in a larger group, I do not allow more than one signature per student on a single sheet. This ensures that students are circulating and speaking to a variety of people rather than having one or two people complete their sheets; this also makes the activity more challenging. If you have a small group, however, you might expand this limit to 2 or more in order for students to have the opportunity to complete the sheet.) Also, determine if students are allowed to add themselves to their own sheet.

If teaching in a physical classroom, be sure to have enough space for students to move around and encourage students who are able to physically circulate the room while also ensuring that students who cannot move around are accommodated by having students come to them. (Also consider additional accommodations such as linguistic and auditory.) **If teaching in a virtual environment,** consider creating breakout rooms where students can freely move around to speak with one another. You can also use the chat function for students to message each other. Share the link to the digital handout and have students download the handout or make a copy if using Google docs. Rather than having students sign each other's sheets, they can simply write down the name of the person that they found.

After distributing the handout to the students, determine if you want to allow time for students to read it over and ask questions or if you want to delve right into the activity. Depending on your time allotment, you can either have students play until the first person (or first few people) has found a person to sign on to each prompt OR set a timer and play until the timer ends. If playing competitively, the person with the most signatures when the timer is up is the winner. (I recommend having multiple "winners" in case some students who signed a sheet are not comfortable showing and proving or if a guideline was not followed, such as one signature per person.) Once you have ended this portion of the activity, it is time for "show and prove."

For the "show and prove" portion, the students who completed their sheets first or had the most signatures before time was called will share the names of their signees who will then be asked to "show and prove" the knowledge or skill that they claimed. Alternate between the winning students to ensure that the people who signed their form can share their knowledge or skills. For some prompts, there will likely only be one student sharing (e.g., finishing the line, "It was all a dream), while for other prompts, it might make sense to have signees collaborate (e.g., perhaps Kayla shares five rappers who are women while Jared shares another five). For performance-based prompts, provided you have the time, it might be more fun to have multiple students "show and prove," especially if some students are really excited to show this skill. If facilitating this activity as a competitive game, the students who had the most signatures or completed the sheet first will receive their accolades once their signees have shown and proven. If resources allow, consider also rewarding the students (signees) who participated in "show and prove" to honor their efforts, vulnerability, and support of their classmates.

It is worth noting that this activity is deliberately vocal and interactive. With or without music playing during the activities, the room will inevitably be boisterous, and this is a good thing. Students *should be* laughing, cheering, whooping, and clapping. To accommodate this, you might want to let the neighboring classes know that you are conducting this activity and that your room might get loud, giving other teachers the opportunity to structure their classroom activities accordingly.

Sample Activity Sheet

(Keep in mind that popular culture and youth culture are constantly in flux; thus, the example shown should guide your development of your activity but should not be used without revision to account for the social, cultural, and geographic contexts of your students.)

Name:

Directions: For each of the prompts below, write the name of the person you found and have them sign. Answers must be truthful and you must use a DIFFERENT person for each prompt (be aware that they may be asked to prove some of these abilities). The first person to complete the form OR whoever has the most signatures when time is called is the winner!

FIND SOMEONE WHO . . .

1. Can name the five elements of Hip Hop

    _____   _____
    (Printed Name)   (Signature)

2. Can perform a TikTok dance

    _____   _____

3. Can recite a whole rap verse

    _____   _____

4. Can name all members of [e.g., Migos, Wu-Tang Clan, City Girls]

    _____   _____

5. Can list at least five Verzuz battles

    _____   _____

6. Can finish the line, "It was all a dream . . ."

    _____   _____

7. Can name ten rappers who are women

_____   _____

8. Can name three rappers from [insert local town/city here]

_____   _____

9. Can freestyle

_____   _____

10. Can list three movies about Hip Hop OR that feature a rapper

_____   _____

Class Playlist

Another activity that can cultivate community amongst your students early in the semester is the development of a class play-list based on students' musical interests. For this assignment, students will select their favorite Hip Hop song and add it to a class playlist that all students can access. This is an independent assignment that can be completed at home; however, the best iteration of this activity involves students presenting their songs in class. In doing so, students are able to discover connections with each other, see their classmates in new and oftentimes trans-formative ways, and provide the teacher with information about students' musical and popular cultural interests, which teachers can then embed into future lessons and curriculum.

I first developed this assignment a few weeks into a high school class that I was teaching as the class was still figuring out its culture and identity. I asked the students to go home over the weekend, select their favorite Hip Hop song, and send it to me by email. They were also asked to be prepared to explain their "why" in class on Monday. Although I had anticipated the students' presentations to take up one class period, the students were so engaged and so eager to share their songs that we ultimately took two class days to complete the presentations. It was during these presentations that I realized how rarely high school students are given space in the classroom to share parts of themselves that fall outside of the standardized curriculum. For many of the students, their identities and stories had not been centered in the classroom since the days of "show and tell" in elementary school. These presentations, then, became an empowering space for the students individually as well as a collective space to explore the fullness of students' humanity.

The favorite Hip Hop song presentations also became a way for me to learn more about my students' stories and identities in ways much more profound than traditional class assignments and in ways that challenged my own biases and assumptions. For example, when one of my students, Sonya, presented her favorite song "Vocab" by the Fugees, I was surprised that she even knew the song, having been released before she was born, much less why she would choose it as her favorite. Sonya explained that she distinctly recalled being in the backseat of the car as her mother blasted this song throughout the streets of Brooklyn, New York, when she was a child. For Sonya, this song was both a connection to her mother and to her childhood neighborhood, which she moved away from and missed dearly.

Another student, Mark, announced at the beginning of the semester that he did not listen to Hip Hop. However, he presented the song "Moment of Truth" by rap group Gang Starr and explained that this song has significance for him since he recalls it from the Dave Mirra Freestyle BMX video game that he played with his brother when they were children and before his brother began a harrowing battle with substance abuse and addiction. As both of these examples reveal, the class playlist assignment is less about the music itself and more about the stories that forge students' identities and connections to the world, their families, and popular media. Recall that these presentations occurred early in the semester and in a class where students' relationships ranged from being best friends, enemies, former friends, or complete strangers. Yet, the space provided for students to share themselves through the lens of Hip Hop music led to students working towards healing through storytelling as well as to the formation of a classroom community that was deeply connected, vulnerable, and honest.

The specificity of this prompt is critical to the success of the assignment. I have experimented with variations of the prompt, such as "your favorite song" and "your theme song" and I have found that the song selections become less deliberate and the stories become less specific the broader the prompt gets. This does not mean that your students should necessarily choose a favorite Hip Hop song; perhaps, based on the cultural context of your students, you decide on a favorite country song, bachata song, or rock and roll song. Whatever you choose, it is important to be specific as it increases both the challenge and profundity of the assignment and its outcomes.

Activity Directions for Teachers

Preparation: First, create an empty playlist that students can access using a virtual platform such as Apple Music, Spotify, or YouTube (the latter two are likely the most accessible for students). Be sure to click on the option to add collaborators (optionally, students can send the songs to you, and you can curate the play-list). Consider having a student volunteer to create and perhaps curate the playlist. By curation, I mean that rather than having the songs randomly appear in the playlist, you or a student can move the songs around so that there is an order to them based on whichever categorizations you prefer, such as tempo, theme, or even chronology. (If you have ever made a mixtape, then you will have had some experience with this process.) Also, decide if there are particular requirements for students regarding language and content. For example, are songs containing certain language "off-limits"? (See the note on "Language and Censorship" in Chapter 1 for details.)

Facilitation: Share the prompt (e.g., What is your favorite Hip Hop song and why?) with students as a homework or classwork assignment and provide a deadline for when the songs are due. Be sure to build in options for students to contribute if they do not have access to resources such as smartphones, computers, internet, etc. (e.g., Perhaps they tell you the song and you can add it, or perhaps a classmate can add it for them.) Remind students that they will be presenting their songs and their "why" in class. (If you do not have time for in-class presentations, perhaps students can post their reasons or post a video of themselves explaining their "why.") Before presentations begin, decide if you want the students to listen to the playlist beforehand to contextualize the presentations; if you want students to listen to the playlist after the presentations in order to contextualize their listening experience; and if you want students to play a snippet of the song before or during their presentations (this takes more time but is typically more engaging for students). Perhaps you pose these questions to the class for a consensus. Also, clarify for the students how long the presentations are expected to be (I recommend 2–3 minutes depending on whether or not they play a part of the song) and what must be included (see what follows for additional ideas).

Assignment Variations

We have discussed here a version of the class playlist assignment that serves to introduce students to the class and to cultivate a classroom community that accounts for students' complex histories and identities. However, this assignment can also be molded to work within particular academic units in your curriculum. For example, if your students are reading and working towards writing personal narratives, perhaps you use this assignment as a lens to jog students' memories and develop the skill of detailed descriptions. To this end, the prompt might include something like, "Describe your earliest recollection of this song. Who were you at that time? What do you remember about that time or that moment? What images, sounds, smells, or memories come up for you when you hear the song now?" Students might embed these responses in their presentations, or perhaps there is a third part of the assignment in which they write a brief paragraph responding to these prompts.

Another variation of this assignment is asking students to add a song to the playlist that responds to the Essential Question or Big Idea of the unit. In this version, consider engaging in a class discussion of the Essential Question or theme of the unit and then assigning for homework that students add to the playlist a Hip Hop song (or song from another genre) that reflects on or highlights this question or their response to the question. Similarly, students could be asked to add songs to the playlist that form a "soundtrack" to the unit. For example, if this book (or unit, historical time) was a movie, what song would you add to the soundtrack and why? Within the students' presentations, you can also include an analysis of the song's themes, literary devices, sonic elements, or other components that correspond to the academic skills embedded in your curriculum. Be mindful, however, that these additional prompts should not supplant the discussion of "why" students chose and connect to a particular song; rather, they should supplement the original prompt such that the assignment still focuses on students' identities and engagement with their social and cultural worlds.

Some Common Core ELA/Literacy Standards Reflected in this Lesson

CCSS.ELA-LITERACY.CCRA.R.1
CCSS.ELA-LITERACY.CCRA.SL.1
CCSS.ELA-LITERACY.CCRA.SL.2
CCSS.ELA-LITERACY.CCRA.SL.5

Lesson Three

"I Used to Love H.E.R.": Exploring Extended Metaphor and Allegory in Hip Hop Literature

In this lesson designed for English language arts and creative writing courses, students learn about the literary devices of allegory and extended metaphor through analysis of two Hip Hop songs. "I Used to Love H.E.R," written by Common and released in 1994, tells the story of a girl that the rapper met as a child and for whom he developed a deep love and respect. As the girl grew older, she developed an Afrocentric mentality and shared messages of peace and non-violence. However, in moving to the West Coast, specifically to Los Angeles, this young woman eschewed Afrocentricity in favor of materialism and expanded her proclivities to become more well-rounded. Eventually, this young woman "sold out," abandoning her creativity in order to gain money and popularity and allowing herself to be used by others to spread toxicity. At the end of the song, Common expresses hope for his future with "H.E.R.," revealing that who he is describing is not a woman at all, but rather the genre and culture of Hip Hop.

Kanye West's "Homecoming," released in 2007 as an homage to Common's "I Used to Love Her," also tells the story of meeting a girl as a child and falling in love with her. Although Kanye and Wendy (pronounced "windy") developed a strong bond throughout the years, Wendy expressed that she was hesitant to be with an entertainer since they have a tendency to use her and then leave. Inevitably, Kanye does indeed leave to pursue his dreams. The two stay in touch, but the relationship is different as Wendy gossips about Kanye, expressing negativity towards him and disappointment that the same children that he abandoned also want to be just like him. Ironically, Kanye misses Wendy and wants to make her proud but feels like he cannot return to her. At the end of the song, Kanye reveals that Wendy is not a woman but the "windy city" of Chicago, his hometown.

Both Common and Kanye's songs are steeped in complex literary devices, which make them ideal texts for cultivating students' skills in literary analysis. These include Kanye's allusions to Common's "I Used to Love H.E.R.," the double entendre of "Wendy/windy," and, of course, the allegories or extended metaphors of each text. Oftentimes, teachers will turn to lengthier works such as George Orwell's (1945) *Animal Farm* to teach the concept of allegory. However, in this lesson, students can explore this literary device through texts that might be more accessible and culturally relevant for them. For example, students connected to Hip Hop or any form of popular culture are likely to have witnessed some sort of shift in the culture over time and likely have opinions about this shift and its implications. This experience can provide a clear access point for students to understand Common's narrative as well as the range of emotions, including hope, which his song expresses. Similarly, students who have experienced moving away from a hometown or school or loving a hometown can connect to Kanye's story in "Homecoming," especially the feelings he expresses, such as guilt, pride, and betrayal. In addition to the more overt themes of the songs, these texts also express ideas about role models, the mistreatment of women, the sacrifices that must be made in pursuit of wealth and fame, and the complex relationships we carry with us from childhood. Thus, there are multiple avenues for literary analysis, class discussion, and personal reflection embedded in these songs. Students' emotional connections to these texts can increase their engagement with the lesson and their capacities for understanding the use of allegory in conveying complex ideas. These two songs can also serve as engaging and culturally relevant mentor texts for students to craft their own extended metaphors.

Having taught this extended metaphor lesson in ELA and creative writing classes, I have found that the lesson tends to resonate with students and leads to creative discoveries in student writing, class discussion, and even students' own critical reflection. For example, after I had taught this extended metaphor lesson one year, a student asked me after class one day if I considered rapper Immortal Technique's (2001) song "Dance with the Devil" to be an extended metaphor intended as a lesson or cautionary tale rather than being an autobiographical account. Seeing this student apply our classroom literary analysis to his consumption of popular media made clear to me how powerful this type of lesson can be for students' literary *and* critical development.

In another instance of teaching this lesson, after I had finished reading Kanye's "Homecoming" with the class and the students re-read the text through the lens of allegory, one student asked, "If this isn't about a girl he was in a relationship with, then who are the kids he left behind?" This student had raised an important query given that, at that point in time, Kanye West was not yet a father. As a class, we discussed who these abandoned children could be, and the students determined that he was referring to youth in Chicago who looked up to Kanye even though he had left the city. This led to a powerful discussion of the parallels between famous artists leaving their communities behind and parents leaving their children to pursue economic success, including discussing the expectations that we have for and place on others, how young people choose role models, and patterns in family structure. As the aforementioned examples convey, both of these songs can serve as powerful classroom texts for literary study and critical reflection.

Suggested Timeline

15–20 minutes: Reading and discussion of first text
15–20 minutes: Reading and discussion of second text
10–15 minutes: Class discussion of texts
(If adding writing component)
1–1.5 Class Periods: Extended metaphor writing
10–20 minutes: Student share writing or exchange writing for peer feedback

This lesson can be extended for several days, depending on how you choose to structure students' textual analysis, class discussion, and/or creative writing. However, avoid dragging the literary analysis of the text out longer than one or two days, as students may lose interest and develop an aversion to studying Hip Hop songs in class.

Materials

◆ Printed out or digital copies of both texts
◆ Optional: Edited/clean or explicit audio version of the songs
◆ Optional: Creative writing prompt if transitioning to extended metaphor or allegory writing

Activity Directions for Teachers

Preparation: Look up the lyrics to each of the songs and decide if you will use the original versions or if you will find or create clean/ edited versions to distribute (see note in Chapter 1 on "Language and Censorship"). Create enough handouts of the lyrics to distribute to students. Also, decide if you will play the songs for the students and, if so, which version you will play and when (e.g., before they read the lyrics, as they are reading, or after).

Facilitation: Start the lesson by introducing the term "extended metaphor" (depending on the level and literary background of your students you might also introduce "allegory") and asking students to define and/or give examples of extended metaphor. Then tell students that you will examine two texts that employ this literary device and prompt them to see if they can discover the extended metaphor in each text (this will be more challenging for students if you replace the words "Hip Hop" and "Chi-town" at the end of each song respectively with a blank space or empty bracket). Be sure to remind students, who are already familiar with these texts, to not reveal the metaphor to the other students. Briefly introduce the first song, including the name of the artist and perhaps the year. Chronologically, Common's song was written first. However, I tend to have students read Kanye's song first since they typically have more familiarity with his music and are more likely to recognize his name, if not the song itself. This increases students' engagement in the lesson so that when we get to Common's song, which is older and less likely to be known to students, they are more invested, especially knowing that this song and person inspired Ye.

Consider whether to have students read the lyrics on their own, read along as they listen to the song or if you or a student (perhaps students can take turns) will read the lyrics aloud. To make this determination, consider the identities, backgrounds, and positionality of you and your students (see note on "Honoring the Full Humanity of Students" in Chapter 1 for details). This decision may also be influenced by whether or not you use edited lyrics or the original, explicit version. After students have read the lyrics to the first song, ask for volunteers to share what they think the extended metaphor is (this works best if you call upon students who are reading/hearing this song for the first time). Once this has been revealed, return to the definition of extended metaphor and discuss how this text tells two parallel stories at once. Complete these same steps for the second song before beginning a larger class discussion of the ideas in the texts. After this lesson, you might move on to reading a lengthier literary work that employs extended metaphor or allegory, or perhaps your students practice writing using these literary devices.

Some Common Core ELA/Literacy Standards Reflected in this Lesson

CCSS.ELA-LITERACY.CCRA.R.1
CCSS.ELA-LITERACY.CCRA.R.2
CCSS.ELA-LITERACY.CCRA.R.4
CCSS.ELA-LITERACY.CCRA.R.9

Lesson Four

Embodied Hip Hop Storytelling

In this lesson, students explore the genre of narrative writing and engage in literary analysis and performance as they collaboratively interpret a series of Hip Hop songs read as literary texts. For this activity, students will work in groups to first read their selected or assigned narrative and then discuss their understandings of the text. In this discussion, students can explore concepts such as theme, plot, characterization, or conflict. Once the group has discussed their understandings of the ideas in the song, they then collaborate on creating and performing a dramatic scene based on the narrative, using as much or as little of the original language of the text to convey the same understandings that they found in the song while shifting elements such as setting, plot, or characterization based on the group's creative interpretation. After presenting their performance to the class, each group will give a brief "talkback," during which they share some of their decision-making processes and answer questions from the "audience."

Through this exercise, students encounter familiar texts in new ways and engage in creativity and collaboration while simultaneously processing their own experiences of the world. Students are also able to practice skills in public speaking, close reading, and literary analysis. The post-performance "talkback" is an important part of this process as it emphasizes "process" over "product" and reinforces the necessity of critical reflection. It also helps students to take pride and ownership over their work in class and to see themselves as creators and decision-makers. The students' creation and presentation of dramatic performances of their assigned text is also a significant component in their development of community and self-knowledge. Since this exercise contains multiple entry points for students (for example, they can take on specific roles as facilitator, director, actor, prop and set designer, etc.), it provides a safe and supportive environment for students to experiment with new skills and discover new talents.

One note of caution with this exercise is to be aware of how students might take this prompt in a direction that leads to cultural appropriation, especially if the identities of the students are disconnected from the identities of the song writers/artists. In addition to discussing cultural appropriation with students and checking in on the group's plans for their performance, you can also preempt this issue by selecting songs that are deliberately reflective of students' social and cultural identities. For example, if the majority of your students are white, you might choose songs from artists such as Macklemore, Invincible, or El-P.

Similarly, if your students come from socioeconomically privileged backgrounds and have not previously engaged in the complex work of reflecting on this privilege and developing empathy for others, their performance of narratives based on economic struggle might come across as disingenuous or derisive. This can be especially harmful to students in the class who do identify with the stories being analyzed. To prevent this, you can choose texts that reflect more universal experiences such as love, jealousy, or triumph.

When facilitated mindfully, this lesson can be both uplifting and healing, challenging students to discover more about their own identities and capacities. For example, students who are typically quiet or have never acted before might take part in the performance rather than staying within their comfort zone. Within the safe space of a Hip Hop engaged classroom (rather than, for example, in the auditorium, on stage, or during a school assembly), students can take these small risks to expand their skills and confidence while simultaneously developing academic skills. Additionally, because the dramatic performance of the text is open to students' interpretation, they have the opportunity to write themselves into the narrative as a mechanism for healing and self-discovery. On multiple occasions when I taught this lesson, I have seen groups retain very little of the original words of the text, preferring instead to create their own poem or dialogue that arrives at a similar theme but based on the experiences and identities of the group members.

While the dramatic performances of these Hip Hop texts are a powerful and visual part of the lesson, what I find most fascinating is the dialogue that students have surrounding the original text. Because students in a group will have varying levels of familiarity with the selected song or with the language and terminology that appear in the song, there is a great deal of peer teaching that occurs throughout the group dialogue. Additionally, working with a popular media text and having the goal of turning this song into a dramatic scene for their classmates increases students' motivation to understand and analyze the text. Thus, I often see students engaged in passionate discussions of the meanings of particular words, lines, and stanzas in the song. The process of turning these songs into dramatic scenes also reveals students' perspectives and ideologies about the world, providing more insight for teachers about who their students are and what matters to them.

Suggested Timeline

20 minutes or 1 Class Period: Group Analysis of Texts
20 minutes or 1 Class Period: Development of Dramatic Performances
20 minutes or 1 Class Period: Group Performances and Talkback

This lesson can take anywhere from 1–3 days, depending on the time available.

Materials

- ◆ Printed out or digital copies of Hip Hop songs (see what follows for suggested texts)
- ◆ Directions and Guiding Questions for Students
- ◆ Optional: Access to the #BARS Medley on YouTube (see what follows for details)

Activity Directions for Teachers

Preparation: Prepare a set of narrative-based Hip Hop songs that students can analyze for meaning and resonance, (I recommend selecting songs that have a clear plot, characters, and/or dialogue so that students have a structure to work from). Be sure to account for any songs containing explicit/mature language. If resources allow, prepare more songs than there will be groups so that students have more choice in text selection; also consider having students recommend songs for the activity.

Consider watching the "#BARS" Medley on YouTube, created by Rafael Casal and Daveed Diggs and filmed in 2016 at the Public Theater in New York (I recommend Volume 2). This medley contains a series of performances by poets and actors who convey the primary themes of classic works of literature such as Sandra Cisnero's *The House on Mango Street*, Mary Shelley's *Frankenstein*, William Golding's *Lord of the Flies*, and Chinua Achebe's *Things Fall Apart* in short poetic/rap performances that reflect more modern and urban contexts. These performances can serve as mentor texts for your students by demonstrating how complex themes in literature can be distilled into short, creative scenes that are critically and culturally relevant for the performers and audience. Students might be interested in watching the entire video, or perhaps you select the performances of books that the students have already read.

Facilitation: Begin the lesson by watching clips from the "#BARS" medley with your students. Facilitate a brief discussion of what they noticed in these performances. Then, introduce your students to the prompt. Depending on the literary background of your students, perhaps review concepts such as theme, plot, conflict, setting, and dialogue before beginning group work. Once students are in groups, either distribute one song (with multiple copies) to each group or have one group member select the song pile for their group.

Students may want to listen to the selected songs. Decide if this is an option you would like to extend (sometimes listening to the song can push students' interpretation in a particular direction, so there are arguments for having students only read the text) and, if so, how to address the cacophony that can ensue with multiple students listening to music at once (e.g., Can they use some form of headphones or perhaps move to a different space such as the hallway?). Consider having students assign roles (such as facilitator, timekeeper, researcher, etc.) and if it would be useful to the students to access the song lyrics and annotations on Genius.com to facilitate their analysis. Make sure that students read through and annotate the text at least once before beginning their discussions of the text.

Once students are moving into the performance development stage of their collaboration, provide multiple options for students to participate based on their needs and comfort (e.g., actor, director, set designer, props and staging, etc.) and clarify where the performance area/s is/are as well as what students have access to in the space (e.g., what they can use as props). Also, remind students to be attentive to language and authenticity, avoiding cultural appropriation or the reinforcing of stereotypes (if possible, circulate the room during the performance planning phase to ensure this is not occurring). Once students have presented, facilitate a talkback and audience Q&A (if time is limited, perhaps this can happen in an online discussion or another virtual forum).

Activity Directions for Students

In a group, you will work collaboratively to first critically read and analyze a Hip Hop text. Discuss the text and the meanings and implications that you derive from it. Then plan a dramatic scene (lines do not have to be written or memorized) that conveys the significant themes or conflicts of the text, similar to the #BARS performances (your performance does not require dancing, singing, or rapping; however, you are welcome to include these elements if you choose). Each group will perform their creative interpretations and provide a brief reflection on their processes during an audience talkback.

Sample Guidelines

♦ After reading the lyrics at least once, look through the annotations on Genius.com.

♦ As a group, discuss your understandings of this story.

- ◆ Who are the people (literally and figuratively)?
- ◆ What are the conflicts?
- ◆ What broader implications or ideas does this text convey?
- ◆ Plan a dramatic scene based on your understanding of this narrative. You may use lines from the original song but are also welcome to create or add your own. *Consider language and authenticity.*
- ◆ Decide who will play what roles in this performance (e.g., actor, director, set designer, props and staging, etc.).
- ◆ Practice the performance.

Guiding Questions for Audience Talkback

- ◆ (For performers) Talk about some of the decisions you made in interpreting this text.
- ◆ (For audience) What ideas, questions, or issues does the performance address?
- ◆ (For audience) What stood out to you most when you watched the scene?

Variations

Depending on who and what you are teaching, you might leave the performance open to other forms of creative interpretation rather than requiring students to create a skit or scene. Some examples of non-skit performances include a spoken word poem, an interpretative dance or non-speaking performance, a song or rap (this should not be students performing the song as is, but rather creating their own original text).

Song Suggestions

Keeping in mind that your students' identities and contexts as well as the unit being studied in class should drive your song selection, next is a list of Hip Hop songs that can work well for group discussion and performance in this lesson.

- ◆ "U.N.I.T.Y." Queen Latifah (1993)
- ◆ "Respiration" Black Star featuring Common (1998)
- ◆ "Love is Blind" Eve featuring Faith Evans (2001)
- ◆ "Kick, Push" Lupe Fiasco (2006)

♦ "White Privilege II" Macklemore (2016)
♦ "I'm Not Racist" Joyner Lucas (2017)

Some Common Core ELA/Literacy Standards Reflected in this Lesson

CCSS.ELA-LITERACY.RL.9–10.1
CCSS.ELA-LITERACY.RL.9–10.2
CCSS.ELA-LITERACY.RL.9–10.3
CCSS.ELA-LITERACY.RL.9–10.4
CCSS.ELA-LITERACY.RL.9–10.5
CCSS.ELA-LITERACY.RL.9–10.6
CCSS.ELA-LITERACY.SL.9–10.1
CCSS.ELA-LITERACY.L.9–10.3
CCSS.ELA-LITERACY.W.9–10.3
CCSS.ELA-LITERACY.RH.6–8.1
CCSS.ELA-LITERACY.RH.6–8.2
CCSS.ELA-LITERACY.RH.6–8.4
CCSS.ELA-LITERACY.RH.6–8.5
CCSS.ELA-LITERACY.RH.6–8.6
CCSS.ELA-LITERACY.RH.6–8.7

Lesson Five

Developing Critical Literacies Through Hip Hop Jigsaw Groups

This lesson draws from the "Jigsaw" strategy to develop students' critical literacies through close reading and discussion of Hip Hop songs that share a similar theme. Typically, in a classroom activity that uses the Jigsaw structure, students are tasked with becoming "experts" over a particular text or concept by working in two different sets of groups to develop, share, and co-construct knowledge. (For example, if students are given a study guide for Chapters 1–5 of a text, a student might work in one group to develop expertise over Chapter 1 and then work with a group of students who all had different chapters to share and compare findings, completing the puzzle, or jigsaw, by combining their specific expertise.) In this lesson, students are tasked with exploring a particular question, concept, or theme through literary analysis and discussion.

First, students meet in their "Home" groups, during which they each choose or negotiate which Hip Hop text they would like to become an expert on based on the list provided by the teacher. Next, students meet in "Expert" groups based on the selected text. In these groups, students read, annotate, and analyze their selected text based on the guiding questions provided by the teacher. These questions may include more concrete concepts such as who, what, where, etc., but should move towards thematic questions through which students explore the essential question of the day or unit through the lens of the text. Once this task is completed, students return to their "Home" groups to share their "Expert" group's findings regarding their text.

After each student in the group has shared out, the "Home" group engages in a discussion of the essential question or theme based on patterns, findings, and understandings across all of the texts. This discussion should also be guided by a set of questions provided by the teacher. Finally, each group will share their group's response to the overarching question or idea based on their discussion. This can take the form of summarizing their discussion or answering the guiding questions based on the time available as well as student interest (depending on how many guiding questions there are, having each group answer every question can become tedious and students may become disengaged). Depending on your curriculum, this lesson might be a precursor to exploring this same Essential Question throughout the unit or engaging in this same exercise structure with a full-length or more complex text.

Within this 1–2 day lesson, students accomplish a number of significant goals. First, students are able to engage in complex, literary discussions with short, digestible texts and with texts that may have more relevance or significance for them than traditional classroom literature. Due to the relevance of popular media in students' lives, they might be more inclined to share and challenge ideas within these group discussions, supporting their development of dialogic and listening skills. Additionally, using the Jigsaw structure for this activity allows for the class to engage with multiple texts at once (similar to literature circles) and for students to see a clear purpose to their work in their "Expert" groups since their "Home" groups are relying on them to return with information that the other group members do not have.

Perhaps most importantly, this exercise encourages students to apply critical lenses and perspectives to popular texts, supporting their critical literacy development while cultivating a critical consumption of popular media outside of the classroom. One example of this development occurred during a Jigsaw lesson that I facilitated in which students analyzed a series of Hip Hop songs to examine the concepts of "wealth" and "value." In response to her "Expert" group's song, "Up All Night," (2010) by Drake featuring Nicki Minaj, one student stated, "I already know what this song is about. It's about having lots of money and spending it." Indeed, the two verses of the song describe purchasing luxurious items easily; however, in the song's chorus, Drake repeats how much he loves his "team" and would die for them. After I pointed this out to the group with the question, "What does the author seem to value most?" the group's discussion grew much more complex with a developing interpretation that the author does not aspire to wealth for the sake of simply having it, but rather for the goal of using this wealth as a mechanism for spending time and sharing gifts with loved ones. Thus, through in-class analysis of a familiar song, this student emerged from the lesson with a more complex understanding of the music that she thought she knew so well.

In a meeting that I had with a former high school student two years after she had taken my class, I asked how her experiences in our class impacted her consumption of Hip Hop music. She responded:

I specifically remember just us hanging out, like me and . . . a few other students. We hung out and it was like. . . . It was always in the back of our minds [that] we were listening to Hip Hop a lot differently and we were analyzing it, so it was a lot better.

I often found students who had previously taken a class with me stopping by my classroom, stopping me in the hallway, or emailing me to ask my thoughts on recent Hip Hop songs or artists or to share with me new artists they were listening to. This revealed to me that analyzing Hip Hop as text in the classroom not only increased students' critical literacies but also served to strengthen the connections between me and my students beyond classroom lessons.

Suggested Timeline

20–30 minutes or 1 Class Period: Expert Group Work
15–20 minutes or ½ Class Period: Home Group Work (Share Out and Discussion)
10–20 minutes or ½ Class Period: Whole Class Share Out and Discussion

Materials

◆ Printed out or digital copies of Hip Hop texts
◆ Directions and Guiding Questions for Students

Activity Directions for Teachers

Preparation: Based on your lesson focus and curriculum, select a series of Hip Hop songs that reflect ideas pertaining to the focal theme or question (in the example that follows, the texts studied all deal with notions of survival). Consider having students send song titles that deal with this question or theme as a homework or volunteer assignment. Make decisions regarding any explicit/ mature language in the text, and make sure there are enough copies for each "Expert" group member. Ensure that you have as many songs as you will have "Expert" groups, keeping in mind that the number of songs will equal the number of students in the "Home" groups. Develop two sets of guiding questions, one for the "Expert" groups to discuss and one for the "Home" groups to discuss, as well as directions for students. List all of the songs being studied on the "Directions" document with corresponding numbers. Consider adding the corresponding numbers to the actual song lyrics before photocopying to make it easier for expert groups to find each other. If resources allow (or if teaching virtually), include the assignment instructions, guiding questions, and the lyrics of all of the texts being studied in the same packet to be distributed; otherwise, organize the printed-out songs in piles in an accessible area of the classroom so that students can find their selected text when ready.

Facilitation: After introducing the prompt and task to students, distribute or post/project/share the activity directions. Leave time for students to ask clarifying questions. Assign or have students choose their "Home" groups and arrange their desks so that they are sitting with these groups. Give students a few minutes to determine who will study which texts. Then prompt students, if necessary, to select their chosen song lyrics from the pile before moving into their "Expert" groups (assigning numbers to each song will help to facilitate this process). A slight rearrangement of chairs and desks may be required for this transition based on your student/group ratio. Be sure to determine the time limit for this activity and consider having students take on roles within the group (e.g., timekeeper, facilitator, etc., keeping in mind that there is no note taker role since all students must be taking notes to bring back to their groups).

As mentioned in previous chapters, decide if and how you will allow groups to listen to the songs, keeping in mind that this will increase the time of the activity and may not be necessary for the task of critical reading and analysis. Once time is called, students should return to their "Home" groups to first share out their "Expert" group findings and then discuss the "Home" group guiding questions. Consider setting a time limit or time suggestion for the share-out to ensure that students have enough time for their discussion (oftentimes, students can become so eager to discuss their specific songs that they do not allot time for a fruitful discussion of the findings across the texts). After time has been called or once it seems that groups are ready to share, have each group share the summary of their discussion or findings. If time allows, spend a few minutes after the share-out to facilitate a whole class dialogue responding to the focal question or concept.

Sample Activity Directions and Texts *(corresponding with the Essential Question: What does it mean to survive?)*

Step One: Establish "home" groups at your tables. Select which person will do a close reading of each text. (Note the corresponding number.)

Step Two: Find others in the room who have the same text choice (using the corresponding number will help). In this new group, conduct a close reading of the selected text, focusing on literary terms that stand out to you as significant, the overall meaning, story, or message of the text, and ways in which a consumer/reader/audience member may interpret the text. As a group, discuss the following questions:

- ◆ What is this song about?
- ◆ What do you learn about the narrator?
- ◆ What does the narrator seem to value?
- ◆ What does this song have to say about the idea of "survival"? (i.e., definitions of survival; examples; what is the cost of surviving; what mechanisms do people rely upon to survive?)
- ◆ Do you agree with the ideas, themes, or messages of this song? Explain.

Step Three: Return to your home groups and share out the discussions you had in the last group. Once you have each shared the ideas you found and discussed in your text, put the texts into conversation with each other by responding to the following questions:

- ◆ How do these songs respond to (agree with/conflict with/exemplify) each other?
- ◆ What do these songs say about survival?
- ◆ If these texts are representative of a culture, what is that culture? What does this culture seem to value? What does this culture seem to resist?

Today's Texts

1. "Laila's Wisdom" Rapsody (2017)
2. "Once an Addict" J. Cole (2018)
3. "Drowning" A Boogie Wit Da Hoodie Featuring Kodak Black (2017)
4. "All that I Got Is You" Ghostface Killah featuring Mary J. Blige, Poppa Wu (1997)
5. "Suicidal Thoughts" Notorious B.I.G. (1994)

Some Common Core ELA/Literacy Standards Reflected in this Lesson

CCSS.ELA-Literacy.RL.9–10.1
CCSS.ELA-Literacy.RL.9–10.2
CCSS.ELA-Literacy.RL.9–10.4
CCSS.ELA-Literacy.RI.9–10.6

Lesson Six

Exploring History, Geography, and Culture Through Hip Hop Lit Circles

This lesson or unit supports students' development of Hip Hop literacies as well as sociohistorical understandings of cultures and communities through the examination of Hip Hop narratives in rap lyrics. Students will work in groups to read diverse Hip Hop texts rooted in particular times and geographic locations. Using internet resources, each group will research the locations referenced in the songs and discuss the social, historical, temporal, and lyrical significance of this place both within and outside of Hip Hop culture. Through research, geographic mapping, critical reading, and discussion, students work collaboratively to contextualize the authors and narratives of these texts through an understanding of the histories, cultures, people, and locations that are embedded in them. Each group then presents their findings to the class through a digital or poster presentation. Figures 2.1, 2.2, and 2.3 show examples of student presentations as a culmination of this collaborative activity.

This lesson is a great way to build students' historical and cultural literacies while also showcasing students' prior knowledge. Each time that I facilitate this activity, there are students who are deeply connected to at least one of the songs or artists in the lesson. Oftentimes, these students add additional insight into their collaborative group work and whole-class discussions based on their prior knowledge, expanding even my own understanding of particular artists and texts. In addition to highlighting student knowledge, this lesson can also reveal areas where students have additional room for growth and development.

FIGURE 2.1 Student Analysis of Nice & Smooth's "Sometimes I Rhyme Slow"

An example of this occurred when I taught this lesson to a group of pre-service teachers during a workshop at a university. In this lesson, one of the collaborative groups analyzed the song "Renee" by the Lost Boyz. This song tells the story of a young man from Queens, New York, meeting a young woman who was a law student at the City University of New York John Jay College of Criminal Justice. Throughout the song, the narrator refers to his relationship reverently as a "ghetto love" and his

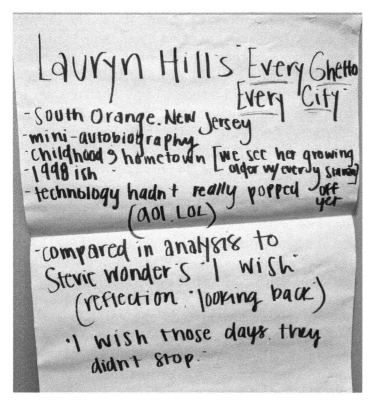

FIGURE 2.2 Student Analysis of Lauryn Hill's "Every Ghetto, Every City"

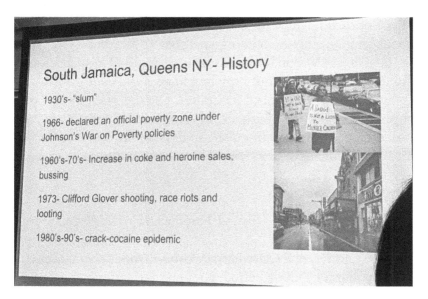

FIGURE 2.3 Student Analysis of Lost Boyz's "Renee"

partner as a "ghetto princess." During the lesson, the group's analysis of the song was presented by a young white woman who was from a suburban town in the U.S. In presenting the analysis, this student repeatedly made references to "the ghetto" and to the song's "ghetto princess," even sharing some of her own experiences working with youth in "the ghetto." Due to the negative connotations of the word "ghetto" as well as the background of the student presenting the group analysis, its use in that particular space and time did not sit right with me.

While I recognized that the song itself used the term "ghetto," it was written by an insider of the community being described and was written in 1996, decades before this lesson occurred and before the term "ghetto" had developed a universally negative connotation, being replaced in the local lexicon by terms such as "hood" which denote a love and celebration of urban culture and community. I also realized that this moment presented an opportunity to make that distinction clear and to remind the students of the complexity of language and the need to differentiate between the language used in particular texts and the language we use to discuss such texts. Ever since that lesson, I began to preempt any discussion of Hip Hop texts in classrooms with a brief discussion about language and its implications. Importantly, such discussions are not specific to Hip Hop texts. I have also had similar classroom discussions about language before reading speeches and texts by historical figures such as Martin Luther King, Jr. Embedded in such lessons are understandings about how language shifts over time, especially in response to social inequities. Lessons such as this one support teachers' and students' development of cultural, historical, sociopolitical, and linguistic understandings in an effort to create more inclusive and socially just communities.

Suggested Timeline

10–20 minutes or 1 Class Period: Introduction to Hip Hop Culture/ Language
30–60 minutes or 1 Class Period: Group Work
30 minutes or 1 Class Period: Group Presentations
20–30 minutes or 1 Class Period: Class Discussion

This lesson can be facilitated in one day or one week, depending on the time available and the readiness level of the students.

Materials

♦   Printed out or digital copies of Hip Hop texts
♦   Chart paper, poster paper, or whiteboard markers and whiteboard space OR shared online folder for group presentations
♦   Directions and guiding questions for students

Activity Directions for Teachers

Preparation: Prepare a set of Hip Hop songs for the students to examine in groups. These songs should explicitly name or reflect a particular geographic location or perhaps a number of locations. You can choose these songs yourself or ask your students for suggestions. Be sure to account for language as well as the geographic, social, and cultural contexts of the students in your class. Prepare enough copies for each of the group members to have a copy of the song; or, if distributing lyrics digitally, prepare digital folders so that each group has a copy of the text and the guiding questions in their folder. If group presentations are digital, create a shared folder for students to upload their presentations. Be sure to predetermine approximately how long the group presentations should be.

Facilitation: Begin with sharing the lesson goals and instructions with the students, including the timeline for each activity. **If teaching in a physical classroom**, organize the classroom so that students are sitting in their groups. Distribute the instructions and Hip Hop texts to each group or consider displaying the song choices on a table in the room and having a representative from each group choose the song for their group. Consider displaying a timer in the classroom so that the students can monitor how much time they have remaining. Circulate the room as students are working to provide support and address any confusion or challenges.

If teaching in a virtual environment, create breakout rooms and assign a text for each room to study. Share the link to the digital presentation and/or folder containing the songs, instructions, and place to upload group presentations. Once the group work time has lapsed, have the groups take turns sharing out their findings with the rest of the class based on the guiding questions and their mapping of the text. Allow time for classmates to ask follow-up questions or contribute additional information or insights after each presentation. After all presentations are complete, facilitate a whole-class dialogue about the students' takeaways from the activity. Consider the following discussion questions to guide this dialogue.

Discussion Questions:

◆ What did these songs teach us about particular cultures, communities, or histories?
◆ What information from today was new or surprising for you?
◆ How does your understanding of these geographic locations impact your understanding of history, Hip Hop, or the narratives of these particular artists?

Sample Activity Directions for Students
As a group, read and annotate the selected text first on your own. Discuss questions that you have about the text, including language and references. Next, look up the text using sites such as Genius.com and read the annotations to add to your understanding of the text. Then use internet resources as well as the knowledge of your group members to discuss and answer the questions that follow. Be prepared to present your findings, including your map, to the class.

1. *Socio-historical and cultural context*
   a. When was this song created?
   b. What was happening sociopolitically at the time?
   c. What types of technology were available? (i.e. AOL, internet, computers, smartphones, etc.)
2. *Geography*
   a. What geographic places are mentioned in this song?
   b. Map these places out visually (perhaps digitally).

3. *What can you learn about this community?*
    a. Who is there?
    b. What is its history?
    c. Is this a famous, popular place? If so, what is its significance?
    d. What changes have taken place in this community over time?
    e. Describe the general economic status of this community.
    f. What public transport (if any) is available? If the song mentions a train or bus, what train or bus would they have taken?
    g. What is particular to this community in terms of language, stores or monuments, famous people, habits?
    h. (How) is this song reflective of this community?
4. *Text Analysis*
    a. What can we learn about the author?
    b. How does the author's history/context influence this text?
    c. What themes are presented in this narrative?
    d. What ideologies does this story support/uphold or challenge?
    e. What ideas from this song do you see present in society or in Hip Hop today?
    f. What ideas seem outdated or non-representative?

Song Suggestions

◆ "South Bronx" KRS One (1987)
◆ "Renee" Lost Boyz (1996)
◆ "Elevators (Me and You)" Outkast (1996)
◆ "Every Ghetto, Every City" Lauryn Hill (1998)
◆ "Brooklyn" Mos Def/Yasiin Bey (1999)
◆ "Georgia" Ludacris f. Field Mob and Jamie Foxx (2005)
◆ "Philadelphia Born and Raised" Meek Mill (2010)
◆ "DC or Nothing" Wale (2011)
◆ "Duckworth" Kendrick Lamar (2017)
◆ "Chrome (Like Ooh)" Rapsody (2017)
◆ "Hoyt and Schermerhorn" Leikeli47 (2018)
◆ "Higher" DJ Khaled f. Nipsey Hussle and John Legend (2019)

Some Common Core ELA/Literacy Standards Reflected in this Lesson

CCSS.ELA-LITERACY.RH.11–12.1
CCSS.ELA-LITERACY.RH.11–12.2
CCSS.ELA-LITERACY.RH.11–12.8
CCSS.ELA-LITERACY.RH.11–12.9
CCSS.ELA-LITERACY.RI.9–10.1
CCSS.ELA-LITERACY.RI.9–10.6

Lesson Seven

Scrubs and Pigeons—Exploring Love and Relationships in Hip Hop Culture

In 1999, the R&B group TLC released the hit song "No Scrubs," which shares a list of qualities and examples that define a person as a "scrub," a "guy" who is broke, ungenerous, and, therefore, unfit to receive love from the songwriters. In response, the rap group Sporty Thievez released "No Pigeons" later that year, a track that parallels "No Scrubs" by defining and sharing examples of "pigeons," girls who are broke and fake and, therefore, unworthy of receiving money or gifts from the songwriters. These two tracks are not alone in representing a subfield of songs within the genre of Hip Hop and R&B music that explicitly describe what the artists or songwriters do or do not want in a romantic partner. Importantly, while rarer, this category also contains songs that reflect standards and expectations for non-romantic relationships. For example, TLC's 1992 song, "What About Your Friends," explores the qualities of true friendships, including loyalty, honesty, and consistency based on the writers' previous hurtful experiences with friends who betrayed and disappointed them.

Drawing from popular media representations of romantic and platonic partnerships, this lesson takes up the discussion of how one develops expectations of love and relationships through close reading and dialogue in response to popular Hip Hop songs. Similar to the activity described in Lesson Five, students will work in various groupings to analyze a set of song lyrics, this time through the lens of love and relationships. First, students will work with a partner to conduct a close reading of one of the songs in the packet, paying particular attention to what the speaker seems to expect of a partner or loved one. Students should annotate the lyrics for evidence of these expectations. Next, students will share out the expectations that they found with the whole class, including the textual evidence that led to their findings. Students will then form larger groups by combining partnerships to engage in a discussion of how these songs express values regarding love and relationships based on the patterns they noticed across the songs and facilitated by guiding questions. Finally, each group will share with the class the values, questions, and understandings that emerged in their small group discussions regarding love and relationships in popular culture.

This lesson is a culturally relevant and engaging approach to facilitating students' critical, social, emotional, and academic development. From a critical standpoint, students are given the opportunity to reflect on the language and representations of relationships in popular media and compare these representations with their own understandings, including how popular media might disseminate inaccurate, unfair, or unhealthy values or expectations of love and relationships. Through a socioemotional lens, this lesson encourages students to examine their own experiences of love and to consider their values as well as how these values developed. Students are also able to practice academic skills in this lesson by conducting a close reading, drawing conclusions based on patterns, and supporting claims with textual evidence. This lesson can be a precursor to additional assignments that engage students in research and dialogue regarding healthy approaches to fostering love and relationships in their lives and communities (see examples at the end of this chapter).

When I taught this lesson in a high school class, the students began to notice patterns across the texts during the partner share-out. One of these patterns was a desire expressed by the women in the texts for their partners to provide material items and financial stability. When we reached the last text, "My Man" by Angie Stone, I asked the students to share the songwriter's expectations from her partner. A student who had not been assigned that song immediately blurted out, "She wants money," based on the developing theme thus far. However, upon reading the lyrics, she immediately followed up with, "Oh, he's a sweet guy . . . he likes her a whole lot, and. . . . She likes her feet rubbed. So she likes being treated right. A structured relationship." Although the class had not yet raised the topic of healthy or unhealthy relationships, the practice of analyzing these texts led to this student's quick recognition of what she deemed as a healthy, or "structured," relationship in Angie Stone's song in contrast to the others we had discussed. Since young people (as well as many non-youth) receive messages through popular media that influence their ideas about what they should seek or value in a relationship, examining this media and presenting counternarratives is a powerful way to support students' agency in developing their own beliefs and resisting those that may be harmful to their health or development.

Suggested Timeline

10–15 minutes: Analysis of selected text
5–10 minutes: Whole-class share-out of findings
15–20 minutes: Small group dialogue across texts
10–20 minutes: Group share-out and class discussion

This lesson can take 1–2 class periods, depending on the amount of students and texts as well as the time available.

Materials

- ◆ Printed out or digital copies of packet containing song lyrics, instructions, and guiding questions
- ◆ Chart paper, poster paper, or white/chalkboard materials and space or shared online document

Activity Directions for Teachers

Preparation: Prepare a packet containing the activity directions, guiding questions, and song lyrics, attending to the language and content of the chosen lyrics. This activity works best if students have access to all of the songs being studied, so consider creating a packet or a single document with all of the lyrics. On the board, on chart paper, or in the online document, create a "T-Chart" with the heading "Expectations" on one side and "Values" on the other.

Facilitation: After introducing the students to the topic or Essential Question of the lesson, have students work in pairs to analyze one or two of the songs in the packet (decide if students will self-select the songs or if you would like to assign or evenly distribute the songs), annotating for the expectations of partnerships or relationships that the songs express. Once time is called, ask for volunteers to share out the expectations that they found, including the textual evidence that led to these findings. Add (or have a student add) the stated expectations to the appropriate column on the t-chart.

Ideally, the students will start to see patterns across the texts during this facilitation. Next, have the pairs join with one or two other pairs to create larger groups to discuss the values that they find across the texts, supported by the guiding questions provided. Once time is called or once groups are ready, have each group share out one or more values that they found across the texts based on the group dialogue. Add these values to the T-chart in the appropriate column. Finally, facilitate a whole-class dialogue about popular representations of love and relationships based on the class notes and discussions.

Sample Activity Directions for Students

Step One: With a partner, conduct a close reading of one of the songs in this packet through the lens of relationships. Create a list of what the speaker seems to value and/or expect of a partner/ loved one. Highlight or underline the lines from the text that you used to draw your conclusions.

Step Two: In a small group, discuss what you noticed across the texts using the guiding questions that follow.

◆ What values do these texts seem to express regarding love and relationships?

◆ Are the values and expectations expressed in these texts similar across gender, sexuality, or other identity markers? Explain. (How are they similar/different?)

◆ What patterns or themes do you find across the songs?
◆ To what extent do the relationships described seem healthy? Typical? Realistic?
◆ Where do these songs challenge dominant stereotypes or representations of gender, power, or sexuality?
◆ Where do these values, ideas, and expectations come from?
◆ The songs in this packet represent __ years of popular rap songs. In reading across them, do you notice any shifts over time in culture, language, or values?

Song Suggestions

1. "Around the Way Girl" LL Cool J (1990)
2. "What About Your Friends" TLC (1992)
3. "All I Need" Method Man f. Mary J. Blige (1994)
4. "Whatta Man" Salt n Pepa f. En Vogue (1994)
5. "Gotta Man" Eve (1999)
6. "No Scrubs" TLC (1999)
7. "I Need a Girl" P. Diddy f. Usher and Loon (2002)
8. "Nothin Out There For Me" Missy f. Beyonce (2002)
9. "You Make Me Better" Fabolous f. Neyo (2007)
10. Your Love" Nicki Minaj (2010)
11. "Love the Way You Lie" Eminem f. Rihanna (2010)
12. "Fancy" by Drake feat. T.I. & Swizz Beatz (2011)
13. "Brothers" Kid Cudi (2013)
14. "No New Friends" DJ Khaled f. Drake, Lil' Wayne, Rick Ross (2013)
15. "We Ride" Gucci Mane f. Monica (2017)
16. "Testify" Future (2017)
17. "Photograph" by J. Cole (2018)
18. "Ring" Cardi B f. Kehlani (2018)
19. "Best Friend" Saweetie featuring Doja Cat (2021)
20. "Mind Yo Business" Lakeyah featuring Latto (2022)

Additional Assignments

◆ Find an elder in your life or community and ask them about their favorite love song.

- ◆ Write a song or poem that reflects your understanding, experience with, hope for (healthy) relationships.
- ◆ Write a short story that imagines a healthy relationship.
- ◆ Conduct a research project that investigates different types of healthy relationships.
- ◆ Create a survey that investigates different types of relationships.
- ◆ Conduct interviews and create a written piece or an informative video that investigates relationship-building.

Some Common Core ELA/Literacy Standards Reflected in this Lesson

CCSS.ELA-LITERACY.RL.9–10.1
CCSS.ELA-LITERACY.RL.9–10.4
CCSS.ELA-LITERACY.RH.9–10.6
CCSS.ELA-LITERACY.SL.9–10.1
CCSS.ELA-LITERACY.SL.9–10.4
CCSS.ELA-LITERACY.CCRA.W.7
CCSS.ELA-LITERACY.CCRA.W.9

Lesson Eight

Developing Critical Hip Hop Literacies Through Standardized Exam Preparation

A frustration that teachers often express in workshops that I have taught on Hip Hop education is that these lessons are incongruous with the expectations of traditional curriculum and standardized exams. However, as previous lessons in this book have shown, teachers can work with media texts in their classrooms in ways that do not sacrifice students' academic development or their ability to succeed on high-stakes tests. In fact, using popular texts in the classroom can support students' development of the skills that such tasks require in ways that are culturally relevant and engaging. In this lesson, students practice skills in literary analysis and thematic writing by examining student-selected popular songs in preparation for the writing component that accompanies many standardized tests in ELA.

Many standardized ELA exams ask students to analyze a short literary text by identifying and analyzing its themes and literary devices. For example, one of the writing tasks on the New York State ELA Regents exam, which was a state requirement for the high school students that I taught, asks students to read a short passage and write a two to three-paragraph response in which they identify a central theme in the passage and provide textual evidence to discuss how the author employs a particular literary or rhetorical strategy in the text to convey this theme. An important component of this exercise is that the text that students analyze on the exam is most likely new and unfamiliar to the students. In comparison to longer works of literature that students study over the course of weeks or longer in the classroom, the passage that the state exam provides asks students to display their competencies in literary analysis and writing without the support of class discussion, teacher feedback, or time. Since this task differs from traditional classroom approaches to literary analysis, it can be daunting for students. In order to prepare my students for this part of the exam, I have them practice in the classroom using popular texts.

Although critical approaches to Hip Hop pedagogy are not intended to reinforce or justify high-stakes testing practices, it is necessary to recognize the realities of teaching in K-12 public schools and the need to prepare students for the structures that they will be facing even as we actively work to challenge and dismantle these structures. This lesson supports students' ability to navigate their realities while simultaneously providing students will tools to interrogate and speak back to these realities. In this two to three-day lesson, students work as a whole class to closely read and analyze a popular song, identifying themes, literary devices, and rhetorical strategies in the text. Then, as a class or in small groups or pairs, students will co-construct a short response to the text that analyzes the author's use of writing techniques. As a homework or classwork assignment, students will identify and either bring into class or send to the teacher song lyrics that can be analyzed for literary devices and meaning.

On the following day, the students will work individually to follow the same steps from the day before to analyze the student-selected song assigned to them, identifying themes, literary devices, and rhetorical strategies in their text. After sharing their findings in small groups, students will then work individually to write their responses to the text based on the guidelines of the standardized exam that they are preparing for. Students may engage in a round of peer review with their groups before submitting their writing to the teacher for feedback.

While teachers who engage with youth popular media might be tempted to select the songs for analysis, having students bring in the texts for their peers to analyze is an important component of this lesson. The process of selecting a song that clearly makes use of literary devices and writing techniques to convey meaning is a challenging exercise that encourages students to read their favorite songs through a critical and literary lens. Consequently, this lesson can provide students with new perspectives for encountering popular texts and for coming to their own understandings of the purpose and impact of art. In teaching this lesson, I have observed students begin to recognize the difference between songs that make use of a wide range of literary devices and those that contain very few. In fact, the students who were most challenged by this exercise were those whose songs either lacked creative use of literary techniques or did not seem to convey a clear message or significance. By no means is this activity intended to reflect or foster judgment towards particular music or artists; rather, this lesson moves students closer to self-actualization as they engage in their own reflections on what moves them sonically, linguistically, and textually.

Suggested Timeline

1 Class Period: Whole-Class Text Analysis and Writing
10–20 minutes or ½ Class Period: Individual Reading and Analysis of Assigned Text
10–20 minutes or ½ Class Period: Group Dialogue (Optional)
20–30 minutes or ½ Class Period: Individual Text Response Writing

Materials

- ◆ Printed out or digital copies of whole-class text
- ◆ Presentable version of whole class text (e.g. on a projector)
- ◆ Printed out or digital copies of directions for students
- ◆ Printed out songs for students to analyze individually

Activity Directions for Teachers

Preparation: For Day One, choose a Hip Hop song (or other popular text relevant to your students' cultures, identities, and interests) to analyze as a whole class. Ensure that this text has a number of clearly identifiable writing techniques, including literary devices and/or rhetorical strategies. This song should ideally be one whose message fosters a healthy and critical discussion with students (see what follows for song suggestions). Depending on the level of your students, consider pre-highlighting some examples to jumpstart the class dialogue of the text. You might also want to pre-write a sample paragraph in response to the text. Prepare a copy of the targeted standardized test directions that students will use, making any adjustments necessary for this lesson. For Day Two of the lesson, be sure to prepare approximately five backup songs for students. This accounts for students who may forget to bring or send their lyrics and for lyrics that are not suitable for the lesson.

Facilitation: Distribute the song lyrics to students and determine if it is useful to play the song or not. After having students read the text or after reading it aloud as a whole class (if this is a popular song, which I recommend, there will likely be students who volunteer to read it aloud to the class), have students identify writing techniques (e.g., literary and rhetorical devices) and highlight these on the text, adding the meanings and interpretations that students come up with, if applicable. Next, facilitate a dialogue about the themes, motifs, and messages that students derive from the text. Discuss with the class how some of the devices that they identified support the development of one or more of these themes. Finally, work as a whole class, in pairs, or in groups to draft one to two paragraphs that analyze the text using the guidelines provided by the standardized test directions.

At the end of class, let the students know that they will work on their own tomorrow to complete this task for a new text. Provide the homework assignment: Choose a song and identify one theme and at least two literary devices or rhetorical strategies in the song. Then email or bring in (if students have access to a printer) the lyrics to a song, writing the devices and theme that they found in the body of the email or on a separate sheet of paper. (It is important that students do not include this information on the actual lyrics.) If you have been editing song lyrics for the classroom or using edited lyrics, be sure to give instructions to your students for finding or creating edited lyrics, including how they will know what type of language is considered appropriate for the classroom and for this assignment.

On Day Two, collect the song lyrics from students, shuffle them, and redistribute them so that none of the students have the song that they brought in. This process helps to mimic the standardized test format in which students do not know what passage they will get and will have to develop a response with limited time and background knowledge. Similar to the standardized test in which no one can guarantee that all students are unfamiliar with the passage provided, some students may have seen their assigned text before, and some will be encountering this song for the very first time. Reassure students that whether or not they know the song already should not impact their success on this assignment. However, if a student expresses that they are distracted by a particular text for any reason, you can switch their text with one of the backup songs that you prepared. Similarly, if a student finds that they cannot identify a clear message or writing techniques in their assigned song (I recommend looking the song over to see if that is accurate), then you can switch this text with a backup song.

After giving students independent time to read and annotate their assigned text, consider if it might be useful for students to meet in small groups to share their findings with others for triangulation and feedback. This dialogue can help students to articulate the connection they are finding between the devices and the song's themes as well as expose the other students to the various songs in the room as well as new perspectives on these songs. Because students might have a lot of familiarity and interest regarding these texts, be sure to circulate the room and ensure that conversations are on topic and students have equal time to share. After this group dialogue, students will return to working individually to develop their constructed response to the text based on the directions and guidelines distributed. Depending on the time available and the needs of your students, consider facilitating a round of peer feedback before having students submit their essays to you, keeping in mind that having students share their writing on media texts with each other expands their access to critical literacies and to diverse perspectives.

Song Suggestions for Whole-Class Analysis

1. "Black Zombies" Nas, (2002)
2. "All Falls Down" Kanye West (2004)
3. "Complexion (A Zulu Love)" Kendrick Lamar (2015)
4. "Summer Friends" Chance the Rapper (2016)
5. "Nina" Rapsody (2019)
6. "Middle Child" J. Cole (2019)
7. "The Bigger Picture" Lil Baby (2020)
8. "My Power" Chika (2020)
9. "Shine" Robert Glasper, D Smoke, Tiffany Gouche (2021)
10. "Aquamarine" Dangermouse and Black Thought featuring Michael Kiwanuka (2022)

In the song "Chaining Day," rapper J. Cole discusses the ways in which material wealth corrupts people who acquire wealth. The use of chains in this song symbolizes one's status, especially within Hip Hop. Wearing a chain shows others that one has "made it," but it also draws envy from others. For J. Cole, his chain makes him feel as though he has succeeded, but he also feels guilty for falling into the trap of greed and materialism. In the song, J. Cole writes, "Money short so this jewelry is like a weave." Through this simile, J. Cole compares signs of material wealth to weaves in that they can both be deceptive and are often used to show off one's status, but they are also temporary and serve to hide a reality. At the end of the song, J. Cole repeats "this is the last time," indicating that he plans to stop wasting his money on superficial signs of success. However, the repetition of the line reveals the cycle in which people often get stuck, wanting to stop their destructive behaviors, but not being able to due to greed and corruption. This idea is further solidified in the title of the song "Chaining Day" which is an allusion to the film Training Day, in which a police officer, usually a symbol of good and innocence, is corrupted by greed and this corruption leads to his downfall. Ultimately, J. Cole expresses the idea that the pursuit of material wealth is a trap that can corrupt and destroy otherwise innocent individuals.

FIGURE 2.4 Whole-Class Analysis of J. Cole's "Chaining Day." Highlighted portions reflect analysis of theme and literary devices

Some Common Core ELA/Literacy Standards Reflected in this Assignment

CCSS.ELA-LITERACY.CCRA.R.1
CCSS.ELA-LITERACY.CCRA.R.2
CCSS.ELA-LITERACY.CCRA.R.3
CCSS.ELA-LITERACY.CCRA.R.4
CCSS.ELA-LITERACY.CCRA.R.5
CCSS.ELA-LITERACY.CCRA.W.1
CCSS.ELA-LITERACY.CCRA.W.2
CCSS.ELA-LITERACY.CCRA.W.4
CCSS.ELA-LITERACY.CCRA.W.5
CCSS.ELA-LITERACY.CCRA.W.10

Lesson Nine

(Re)Defining the Modern Hip Hop Generation Through Critical Media Literacies

Too often, young people find themselves responding to the pressures that adults place on them based on outdated conceptualizations of what it means to be young and what it means to be successful in our world. In spite of the immense transformations that our society and those within it have endured as a result of the multiple pandemics (e.g., health, racial, economic, climate, etc.) since 2020 (Ladson-Billings, 2021), youth in schools continue to be held to standards and structures that fail to reflect who they are, what they need to thrive in our ever-shifting world, or how to proactively build towards their social futures (Mirra & Garcia, 2022). Writer and activist Audre Lorde (1984) once stated that "if we do not define ourselves for ourselves, we will be defined by others—for their use and to our detriment" (p. 45). This is especially so for youth of color and marginalized youth who are rarely provided opportunities for self-definition in schools or in society. In order to best teach today's youth and most effectively support their ability to understand and take action within their social worlds, educators should work with students to collectively reflect on modern youth culture and identity.

In 2002, Bakari Kitwana defined the "Hip Hop Generation" as Black Americans born between the years 1965 and 1984 who were the first generation to develop outside the structures of legal segregation (Kitwana, 2002). Kitwana's definition inevitably includes a discussion of racial and class divisions, the war on drugs, and the vulnerability of youth of color, particularly in urban areas. As Dimitriadis (2009) explained, it was during this time period that "hip hop emerged against all logic and against all odds as the preeminent expressive form for contemporary youth" (p. xxii). Now, more than 20 years later, Hip Hop music and culture continue to be the preeminent force of youth culture and popular culture across the world. Yet, Kitwana's definition no longer describes the majority of those currently creating and consuming popular Hip Hop culture. In this lesson, students will explore popular media texts to co-construct understandings of what Hip Hop means, looks like, and sounds like for youth today and to arrive at definitions of the modern Hip Hop Generation that are reflective of young people's current realities.

The overarching questions of this activity are a) Who are the youth of today? b) What has the current generation of youth inherited? c) How do today's youth envision their futures? And d) What do today's youth need to build towards the healthy and successful futures that they envision? This lesson begins by examining historical definitions or conceptualizations of Hip Hop and the Hip Hop generation and discussing themes and patterns across classic 80s and 90s Hip Hop texts. Then students will consider the factors that have shaped their generation, including influential events and technology. Next, students will work in groups to examine a set of Hip Hop songs and videos that are representative of current youth popular culture, subsequently creating a written reflection of what they noticed and are considering regarding their identities and youth culture. Finally, students will work to (re)define the Hip Hop generation, drawing from their reflections and discussions. Based on these definitions, teachers should consider how their classroom lessons and curriculum can continue to support their students' developing identities through the introduction of artifacts and theories that cultivate youth agency.

An important component of this lesson is the necessity of teachers reflecting on their understandings of youth culture and popular culture *with* students rather than independently. As an educator, I have found that my perceptions of youth and their engagement with media can be wildly distinct from young people's own perceptions of themselves and their culture. One example of this occurred when I was teaching a group of students who wanted me to watch the music video for the song "Birthday Song" by rapper 2 Chainz featuring Kanye West. When the students played the video in class, I was uncomfortable with how exploitative and misogynistic the song and video appeared to me. I immediately projected that perception onto my students, wondering aloud why they condoned this messaging. Through dialogue, however, I discovered that what these students gravitated towards was not the song's expressions of misogynoir but rather its expressions of power. As high school students, many of whom were youth of color, these students felt disempowered in their daily lives and craved media that allowed them to explore, however vicariously, instantiations of power and abundance. Thus, if we enter classrooms with our own definitions of youth rather than seeing the world through young people's eyes, we run the risk of further silencing our students and limiting their growth and agency in our classrooms.

Suggested Timeline

20–30 minutes or 1 Class Period: Examination and discussion of 80's-90's Hip Hop generation

5–10 minutes: Brainstorming of modern youth generation's influences

30–40 minutes or 1 Class Period: Group discussion of modern Hip Hop texts

5–10 minutes: Individual written reflection (Optional)

10–20 minutes: Co-construction of definitions of new Hip Hop generation and discussion

This lesson can take 2–3 class periods, depending on the amount of time available.

Materials

♦ Printed out or digital copies of song lyrics
♦ Printed out or digital copies of quotes from Bakari Kitwana's book, *The Hip Hop Generation* (2002); instructions; and guiding questions (Optional)
♦ Links to the videos of the selected songs, made accessible to students or ready to play on in-class devices
♦ Chart paper, poster paper, or white/chalkboard materials and space or shared online document

Activity Directions for Teachers

Preparation: Consider reading Chapter 1 of Kitwana's (2002) book *The Hip Hop Generation* and selecting quotes to share with students that are representative of the time period and of Kitwana's definition. These excerpts can be made available for students on handouts, through a shared digital document, or through class slides. Choose a set of Hip Hop texts (songs with accompanying videos) that are reflective of the 80s and 90s Hip Hop generation (be sure to select texts that are attentive to the geographic and cultural contexts of your students) and make these texts available to view in the classroom. Finally, select (or have students select or suggest) a series of recent and popular songs with accompanying videos for group work. Set up the classroom into workstations such that each group is analyzing either the lyrics or the video for one of the selected songs. (If you would prefer for each group to analyze both the lyrics and the video for their song, be sure to allow time for this extended analysis.)

Facilitation: Begin by introducing the purpose of the lesson and the Essential Questions being explored. Next, if using excerpts from Kitwana's (2002) book or a similar text, examine and discuss previous descriptions of the Hip Hop generation. Rooting their understandings of Hip Hop in the sociopolitical context through which it was born will help students to better grasp the historical resonance of Hip Hop as a form of culture, expression, and activism as well as how this culture has shifted over time.

Next, as a whole class, watch and listen to a selection of Hip Hop music videos that are reflective of the Hip Hop generation of the 80s and 90s (see the following suggestions), noting the patterns that stand out to them visually, sonically, and lyrically. (If time allows, consider also reading the lyrics to these songs to increase attentiveness to the lyrical content.) Facilitate a whole class discussion of what students noticed across the examples of the previous Hip Hop generation, discussing visual, sonic, and lyrical elements. As a class, create a list of the themes, patterns, and values that came across in these representative texts.

Transition into a discussion of the current youth/Hip Hop generation by first having students work either individually or with a partner to brainstorm responses to this prompt: "What events and inventions have most influenced your generation?" Consider providing an example or two (such as smartphones and reality television) to jumpstart students' brainstorming. Next, have students share out as a whole class and create a list of these inventions and influences (if teaching virtually, this can occur in a digital, shared document). Once the share-out is complete, highlight a few items on the list and facilitate a dialogue in which students discuss how these items have been influential for their generation.

Provide the prompt for the next part of the lesson: "Watch the video or read the lyrics provided at your workstation. Take notes on what stands out to you in this song or video. What ideologies, values, or practices do you see reflected?" Divide the class into groups and have each group move to a workstation to conduct their group analysis. Remind students to keep the videos on mute so as not to disturb group work and dialogue. After time has been called, have each group share out their findings. Consider playing the video or a clip of the video to provide more context for the other students before each group shares out. Next, have students write individual reflections on what they noticed or what they are thinking about youth culture, popular culture, Hip Hop culture, and/or themselves after experiencing these texts and discussions. Finally, have students work in their groups once again to co-construct a definition of the current youth generation or Hip Hop generation (if time is limited, this can be a whole-class activity), ending class with a share-out of these definitions and whole-class discussion if time allows.

Suggested Songs for Previous Hip Hop Generation Discussion

♦ Public Enemy, "Fight the Power" (1988)
♦ NWA "Straight Outta Compton" (1988)
♦ Queen Latifah, "U.N.I.T.Y" (1993) or "Ladies First" (1989)
♦ Stop the Violence Movement, "Self-Destruction" (1989)
♦ De La Soul, "My, Myself, and I" (1989)
♦ Slick Rick, "Children's Story" (1988) or "Hey Young World" (1988)
♦ Salt 'n' Pepa, "Let's Talk about Sex" (1990)
♦ Another Bad Creation, "Playground" (1991)
♦ Leaders of the New School, "Case of the P.T.A" (1991)
♦ Arrested Development, "Tennessee" (1992)
♦ 2Pac, "Keep Ya Head Up (1993)
♦ Wu-Tang Clan, "Protect Ya Neck" (1993)
♦ Notorious B.I.G., "Juicy" (1994)
♦ Bone Thugs n Harmony, "Crossroads" (1995)
♦ Jay-Z, "Dead Presidents" (1996)
♦ Nas featuring Lauryn Hill, "If I Ruled the World" (1996)

Some Common Core ELA/Literacy Standards Reflected in this Lesson

CCSS.ELA-LITERACY.RL.11–12.2
CCSS.ELA-LITERACY.W.9–10.1
CCSS.ELA-LITERACY.W.9–10.9
CCSS.ELA-LITERACY.SL.9–10.1
CCSS.ELA-LITERACY.SL.9–10.4
CCSS.ELA-LITERACY.RH.6–8.2
CCSS.ELA-LITERACY.RH.6–8.6

3

Remixing Classroom Assessments

A disconnect that often occurs within Hip Hop education practice is that students are exposed to innovative classroom lessons and culturally relevant texts that reflect their cultures, identities, and outside-of-school practices; yet classroom assessments—the assignments that ultimately determine students' grades and evaluations—remain unchanged. As a result, students may be hesitant to fully engage in Hip Hop-based pedagogies since they will not be assessed on this form of learning. Instead, many students will choose to reserve their investment for classroom activities that impact their grades and, based on traditional structures of schooling and evaluation, their futures. Additionally, excluding Hip Hop and popular culture from classroom assessments sends a message to students that their cultures and identities are acknowledged but not taken seriously within the context of their schooling. Limiting engagement with Hip Hop and popular culture to certain parts of students' learning while keeping traditional forms of assessment intact also contradicts the effort of Hip Hop education to challenge disempowering structures of schooling. Thus, Hip Hop education can only be enacted as a transformative, social justice pedagogy if it is incorporated across *all* aspects of students' learning.

In this chapter, we explore strategies for developing formative and summative classroom assessments that reflect curricular standards as well as students' identities and engagement with popular culture inside and outside of the classroom. These

DOI: 10.4324/9781003293767-3

assignments help students to build essential academic skills in preparation for school-based and standardized testing at the same time that they encourage students to explore their individual and cultural identities and develop critical understandings of the world.

Assignment One: Mixtape Project

This project offers an innovative approach to an end-of-unit, summative assessment that gauges student learning in a way that intersects with students' complex identities and engagement with popular media. Based on the questions, concepts, themes, and ideas that were studied in a particular unit, students work individually to construct a "mixtape," (in most cases, this will be a playlist) containing songs carefully selected to reflect the student's understandings from the unit. Along with the completed mixtape or playlist, students will also submit a written component that explains how each of the selected songs responds to the questions and ideas of the unit.

In order to successfully complete this assignment, students must be able to synthesize the important concepts from the unit as well as critically analyze popular songs. Thus, this assignment assesses students' content knowledge along with their critical media literacy skills. Additionally, this assignment encourages students to critically engage with the music that they are already consuming and to examine the intersections between their cultures and identities and their in-school learning. This assignment also gives teachers an opportunity to learn more about their students and gain insight into young people's popular media engagement. If time allows, students can present their mixtapes in small groups or to the whole class. This project provides a culturally relevant, youth-engaged, and rigorous assessment that can be applied to a majority of curricular units across academic subject areas.

Directions for Teachers
Determine the best format for students to create and submit their mixtapes. In most cases, having students create and share a

playlist on a streaming platform such as Spotify or YouTube will be most efficient. However, if students do not have access to such platforms and do have access to a device that can burn cd's (copy digital files to a blank compact disc), the teacher should distribute blank cd's to the students in advance of this assignment so that students can create their mixtape on the cd and submit to the teacher. The written component of this assignment can be submitted physically or digitally, depending on the classroom structures and resources, as well as the teacher's needs. Include in your assignment description the number of songs that students should submit as well as the estimated length and requirement for each of the song explanations in the written piece.

Towards the end of your academic unit, or perhaps earlier in the unit, introduce this assignment to students to give them time to ruminate on the ideas of the unit and what songs they might like to select. Consider modeling the assignment for your students by creating a few examples of songs that you would select for this assignment as well as your explanation for why or how these texts reflect or correspond to the unit. Be sure to emphasize that students should be selecting texts based on their musical interests rather than those of the teacher. Also, clarify for students what the limits are on what types of songs they can add to their mixtape (e.g., are there restrictions on content or language). Note that the students' processes of selecting songs and considering the appropriate language and subject matter based on these guidelines is also a part of students' critical and digital media literacy development. Finally, since this assignment might be new and unfamiliar to students compared to more traditional assessments, be sure to create an assignment sheet and/or rubric that clearly outlines the requirements and expectations.

Sample Assignment Directions for Students

Task: This project is an assessment of your understanding of the questions, concepts, themes, and ideas that we have studied and discussed in this unit. Based upon your understandings and interpretations of the texts and topics from class, your task is to make a mixtape or playlist of ten tracks according to the requirements that follow. For each of the ten tracks, write a paragraph that explains how the song connects to, reflects, discusses, or responds to the ideas/questions of the unit. It should be clear from your selection and explanation of the songs that you have reflected on the relevant themes and can identify lyrics that reflect these themes in popular music.

Limitations: You may use any song that you find relevant but cannot use any songs that were already studied in class for that particular unit.

Materials for Mixtape/CD: A blank cd and case will be provided to you. Songs should be chosen from your personal song library or music from the public library.

Some Common Core ELA/Literacy Standards Reflected in this Assignment

CCSS.ELA-LITERACY.W.9–10.2
CCSS.ELA-LITERACY.W.9–10.6
CCSS.ELA-LITERACY.W.9–10.9

Assignment Two: Literary Allusions

The literary device of allusion (an implied or indirect reference to a preexisting entity) is often taught in secondary literature and writing courses to support students' reading comprehension as well as their abilities to integrate literary, historical, and cultural knowledge into their writing. Within these lessons, students are often asked to recognize how one literary work references a previous text or a historical or mythological figure or tale. Occasionally, students are exposed to popular media texts in the classroom that allude to canonical literary works, such as the 2004 film *Mean Girls* referencing Shakespeare's *Julius Caesar* or the 1995 film *Clueless* deriving from Jane Austen's novel, *Emma*. Exposing students to the use of allusion in familiar and popular texts is a powerful way to reinforce students' skills in recognizing literary devices as well as to highlight the influence of these devices on students' lives and popular media consumption. In fact, possessing nuanced understandings of literary devices can provide students with additional lenses and frameworks for understanding and acting upon their social worlds.

In this assignment, students explore how allusion functions in creative works by combing through Hip Hop songs (depending on the context in which you are teaching, you might open this up to any music that students are already listening to) for instances of allusion to previous songs (depending on the unit that you are studying in class, you might revise these parameters to include a discussion of literary and/or historical allusions contained within the song rather than allusions to previous songs). Students will then compare the original text to the song that references the original in a written or oral presentation based on the guidelines provided by the teacher (see example that follows).

For this project, students should be aware that allusion can occur in multiple forms, such as referencing a previous work's style, structure, plot, or characters. Chapter 2 in this book provides one example of this in that Kanye West's song, "Homecoming," alludes to Common's song, "I Used to Love H.E.R" in both the format of extended metaphor and in the use of some of Common's lyrics. In the case of music specifically, allusions can also take place through the use of a previous work's sonic qualities or structure. For example, one song might sample or use the same beat as a previous song. Within this assignment, students can analyze the selected texts for accuracy, meaning, structure, style, creativity, or a host of other factors depending on the course goals and curriculum.

This assignment is one that developed organically based on discussions that occurred in a high school class that I was teaching. Within this class, I noticed that students were often unaware of the musical roots of particular songs or artists that they admired, taking an ahistorical approach to their understanding of popular music. This assignment, then, combines students' literary analysis with an exploration of the historical and cultural lineage of the popular texts that influence their lives and perspectives on the world. This assignment provides students with more complex and layered understandings of art, music in particular, that deepens their knowledge of multiple histories and cultures. This assignment is especially useful for adolescents who are in the process of figuring out their own identities as well as how these identities fit into the social structures of their schools and communities.

In my time teaching high school students, I have found that young people often feel immense pressure to solidify their identities, to "know" who they are, and announce that identity through mediums such as college application essays, cafeteria lunch tables, and fashion choices. This pressure to have their identities streamlined and "figured out" can increase students' feelings of anxiety, displacement, and loneliness. Since this assignment reveals the fluidity and interconnectedness of musical genres (e.g., rap songs sampling punk rock songs and vice versa) as well as the importance of history on artistic creation, it contradicts the myth that youth need to essentially choose a "lane" by ascribing to a particular identity group or becoming an expert in one particular field. This assignment also gives students an opportunity to display their cultural and historical knowledge. When students in my class presented their literary allusion projects, I was surprised by the depth of knowledge that some of the students had of music that preceded their time on earth. At the same time, the process of juxtaposing and analyzing their selected songs encouraged students to grapple with the question of what art should *do* for individuals, communities, and society, an important component of students' critical literacy development and activism.

Examples of Allusion in Hip Hop Songs

1. "Children's Story," Slick Rick (1988); "Children's Story," Black Star (1998)
2. "The World is Yours," Nas (1994); "Dead Presidents," Jay-Z (1996)
3. "Killing Me Softly with His Song," Lori Lieberman (1972); "Killing Me Softly with His Song," Roberta Flack (1973); "Killing Me Softly with His Song," The Fugees (1996)
4. "Guantanamera," Joseíto Fernández (1929) [based on the poems of José Martí's "Versos Sencillos" (1891)]; "Guantanamera," the Sandpipers (1966); "Guantanamera," Wyclef Jean featuring Lauryn Hill, Celia Cruz, and Jeni Fujita (1997)

5. "Amores Como El Nuestro," Jerry Rivera (1992); "Deja Vu (Uptown Baby)," Lord Tariq and Peter Gunz (1997) [also samples Steely Dan's (1977) "Black Cow"]; "Dance Like This," Wyclef Jean featuring Claudette Ortiz (2004) [also sampled in Shakira featuring Wyclef Jean, "Hips Don't Lie" (2005)]
6. "Georgia on My Mind," Ray Charles (1978);"Georgia," Ludacris and Field Mob featuring Jamie Foxx (2005)
7. "Harder, Better, Faster, Stronger," Daft Punk (2001); "Stronger" Kanye West (2007)
8. "Why Can't We Live Together," Timmy Thomas (1972); "Hotline Bling," Drake (2015)
9. "X Factor," Lauryn Hill (1998); "Nice for What," Drake, (2018)
10. "Genius of Love," Tom Tom Club (1981); "Fantasy," Mariah Carey (1995); "Big Energy," Latto (2022).

Sample Assignment Directions for Students

Choose a Hip Hop song that alludes to (references) a previous song OR a song that alludes to a previous Hip Hop song. The reference can be based on any of the following: beat, sample, content, chorus, structure, or concept. After analyzing each text, evaluate the efficacy of the second text (the song referencing the original) in terms of the following:

◆ Artistic merit
◆ Honoring of the original text
◆ Innovation
◆ Ability to convey significance

Create an oral presentation that shares both texts and your analysis to the class, including your response to the essential question: *How do these texts have resonance and significance for art, society, and/or Hip Hop culture?*

Some Common Core ELA/Literacy Standards Reflected in this Assignment

CCSS.ELA-LITERACY.CCRA.L.3
CCSS.ELA-LITERACY.CCRA.L.5

CCSS.ELA-LITERACY.CCRA.SL.2
CCSS.ELA-LITERACY.CCRA.R.1
CCSS.ELA-LITERACY.CCRA.R.2
CCSS.ELA-LITERACY.CCRA.R.5
CCSS.ELA-LITERACY.CCRA.R.6
CCSS.ELA-LITERACY.CCRA.R.7
CCSS.ELA-LITERACY.CCRA.R.8
CCSS.ELA-LITERACY.CCRA.R.9

Assignment Three: Hip Hop Literary Criticism

In advanced secondary ELA courses, students are typically exposed to literary criticism, the practice of reading literature through the lens of literary and theoretical frameworks. Examples of literary theories include psychoanalytic, Marxist, post-structuralist, post-colonial, feminist, and Afrofuturist. After learning about literary theories, students can practice applying these theories to their study of literature, providing an opportunity for students to engage in complex theoretical analysis as well as to develop understandings of how particular perspectives impact the interpretation of texts and ideas. Scholars such as Appleman (2014) have advocated for the development of students' critical literacies by applying literary theories to the study of media texts, such as images and videos, in the classroom. As a form of critical media literacy, this practice reinforces the notion that *all texts* are embedded with messages worthy of analysis, even those not traditionally studied in classrooms. By applying critical theories to media texts, students can develop tools for challenging controlling ideas and images (Collins, 2009) in popular media as well as for creating new texts as a form of agency and future-building.

For this assignment, students choose a Hip Hop song and develop a critical analysis by exploring features such as its themes, use of literary devices, language, purpose, and impact. Students with access to the language of literary or critical theories can apply these critical lenses to their analysis of the text, discussing how particular ideologies are implicitly and explicitly

The Look of Lust – Omen Ft. Kendrick Lamar & Shalonda

In this song, Omen tries to put to words his feelings, or lack thereof, for a certain special lady. He is rather honest about being clearly uninterested in the woman's surprisingly strong personality, though he does acknowledge it. Unlike most rap songs, though, The Look of Lust attempts to romanticize what would otherwise be vulgar. The woman 'can feel the rhythm as [he gives her his] guitar licks' as opposed to say, thrusting. She apparently 'never knew [he] was an artist,' which could either me she never knew the man she was sleeping with was a well-known rapper or she never knew how artistic he was sexually. This is all very well but then again it's fairly suspicious that he notes how he only 'plays the instrument well in a dark lit room' and asks if she's 'ever seen a flower in the darkness bloom?' This is perhaps a question of his confidence and masculinity. Perhaps Omen is

FIGURE 3.1 Student's Feminist Criticism of "The Look of Lust" by Omen featuring Kendrick Lamar and Shalonda

conveyed in the song. In addition to the traditional written essay, options for completing this assignment can include creating a class presentation, podcast, song, poem, or blog post.

Engaging in literary criticism through Hip Hop texts can not only support students' academic skill development but can also foster dialogue about how dominant ideologies in history and in society can become absorbed by popular culture and reflected in its music and imagery. Similar to the literary allusion project, this assignment can reveal to students the lineage (ideological in this case) that begets the music they consume and which influences their realities. For example, students in my classes have written research papers in which they discuss concepts such as masculinity, misogyny, classism, and mass incarceration through analysis of the lyrics of Hip Hop songs that they chose. In doing so, many students engage in a more critical reading of the popular music that they consume and oftentimes apply this reading to future texts that they encounter.

Sample Directions for Students

Task: For this project, you will choose a Hip Hop song and analyze its use of literary devices, language, themes, characters, plot, and/or concepts through the lens of one or more critical literary theories as discussed in class. Be sure to include quotes from the text in your analysis and use specific theories and examples to deconstruct and discuss the song. For this assignment, you will create a product (a written piece, song, visual presentation, etc.) to share your analysis and present a piece or a summary of your analysis in class.

Some examples of ways to analyze the song:

◆ What themes are present in the song? Are these themes supported by the examples or evidence in the song? Are these themes consistent with what we see in other songs or in society?

◆ Who is the most likely audience for this song? Is the song appropriate for this audience? Why or why not?

◆ How is the information in the song presented? Is it believable? Is the presentation purposeful? Ironic? Is this presentation effective? In what way?

◆ Are there collaborators in this song? How do they contribute (or take away from) the meaning, presentation, and effect of the song?

◆ Could this song have been presented in a more effective way? If so, how?

◆ What is your interpretation of this song? Is this the meaning that you think the artist hoped to convey? Explain.

◆ How does this song challenge, reflect, or reimagine existing structures, patterns, or behaviors in society?

Some Common Core ELA/Literacy Standards Reflected in this Assignment

CCSS.ELA-LITERACY.CCRA.R.1
CCSS.ELA-LITERACY.CCRA.R.2
CCSS.ELA-LITERACY.CCRA.R.3
CCSS.ELA-LITERACY.CCRA.R.4
CCSS.ELA-LITERACY.CCRA.R.5
CCSS.ELA-LITERACY.CCRA.R.6
CCSS.ELA-LITERACY.CCRA.R.7
CCSS.ELA-LITERACY.CCRA.R.8
CCSS.ELA-LITERACY.CCRA.R.10
CCSS.ELA-LITERACY.CCRA.W.1
CCSS.ELA-LITERACY.CCRA.W.4
CCSS.ELA-LITERACY.CCRA.W.6
CCSS.ELA-LITERACY.CCRA.W.7
CCSS.ELA-LITERACY.CCRA.W.9

Assignment Four: Hip Hop Author Study

The author study is a traditional assignment in ELA classrooms in which students research a particular author by closely examining their life and work, analyzing the intersections between these two as well as noting patterns across the author's writing techniques, themes, and characters. This assessment reflects students' understandings of how literature is influenced by the people and contexts that create it, as well as their ability to identify themes and patterns in literature. For this assignment, students engage in an author study of a particular Hip Hop artist, learning about the artist's life and conducting a close reading of several of the artist's texts. Similar to the traditional author study, this assignment asks students to examine how the author's writing may be influenced by the author's life experiences as well as examine themes, characters, and writing techniques across the author's works.

For this assignment, students can choose a particular artist or album to study. Alternatively, the teacher can assign a particular artist or album for all of the students to study, reinforcing the idea that the same text can contain a multitude of themes and that a reader's perspectives will impact what messages they find. In order to support their findings regarding the themes or ideas that are consistent across the artists' work, the students will write an essay or create a presentation that uses textual evidence to exemplify the themes identified.

When I introduced this assignment to my students, they worked in pairs to conduct an author study of a Hip Hop artist of their choice and create a class presentation that discussed the artist, their work, and the patterns that they saw across the two. One group chose to study the rapper and activist MC Lyte. In their study, these students identified what they deemed to be a "discrepancy" between Lyte's lyrics and the messages of feminism and empowerment that she expresses in her interviews and speeches. In reconciling this misalignment, the students discussed the emergence of Lyte's feminism over time in conjunction with her own journey of self-discovery. Another group examined how the life experiences of rapper Azalea Banks influenced her lyrics as well as her audience. In these presentations, it was evident that students gravitated toward artists whom they felt both connected to and curious about. Engaging in this author study allowed them to consider their own developing identities as well as the complexity of identity for minoritized and historically oppressed communities.

This assignment is especially significant for students who closely identify with popular culture since it provides an opportunity to reflect on the themes and messages that dominate the music that they listen to as well as to develop nuanced understandings of the difference between music as art and music as entertainment. Perhaps most importantly, this assignment can engender meaningful conversations about the notion of "realness" or authenticity in the classroom, a topic that is prevalent for adolescents who are in the process of forging and trying on identities.

Young people, and listeners in general, often have a tendency to map the lyrics of popular artists onto the artist's life, assuming that their work is autobiographical. With rap music in particular, there is an expectation that artists are rapping about their lives and experiences (Rose, 2008). For example, popular rapper Rick Ross, whose artist name derives from the former head of a billion-dollar drug empire, "Freeway" Rick Ross, first rose to fame with his 2006 debut single, "Hustlin'," which boasts about being a successful drug dealer. Two years later, Ross's authenticity was called into question after a photograph surfaced of Ross's time as a correctional officer (Patton et al., 2013). Many accused Ross of being disingenuous since his lyrics were incongruent with his actual life. Years later, popular artist Drake was also accused of being inauthentic when he rapped about "catching a body" (killing someone) in his song "Headlines." A child actor from a middle-class neighborhood of Toronto, Canada, Drake found himself needing to justify his lyrics to an audience that expected his words to match his reality (Scott, 2011). Interestingly, white rappers such as Iggy Azalea and Bhad Bhabie have not been subject to the same amounts of outrage over the disconnect between their lyrics and their realities,[1] perhaps because of an inherent assumption that their artistry is indeed a performance and not expected to be autobiographical.

Since consumption of popular media can lead to the absorption of inaccurate and perhaps harmful messages about identity, especially regarding youth of color in the U.S. (hooks, 2001; Richardson, 2006; Rose, 2008), introducing a Hip Hop author study in the classroom can open up transformative dialogues about race, culture, and identity that can impact students' daily lives and futures.

Sample Directions for Students

For this project, you will work with a partner to analyze a particular Hip Hop artist's work and personal story. The purpose of this project is to reflect on the intersections between one's history and art, including how and why particular themes emerge across an author's work. You will need to choose a Hip Hop artist and find biographical and autobiographical accounts of that artist's life through texts such as memoir/autobiography, interviews, or other written pieces by or about the artist that tell a true story about their life. Then you will select five songs written by that artist that are exemplary of their work. Within the chosen songs, identify lines, stanzas/verses, or stories to analyze through the lens of what you have learned about the artist's life story. Once you have found and analyzed these sources, create a class presentation that shares your findings regarding the artist's life, writing, themes, and artistry. Your presentation should be 8–10 minutes in length and may include any songs, images, or other texts and media that you see as relevant to the presentation.

Suggestions for Whole-Class Study of an Artist

1. 2Pac/Tupac
2. Notorious B.I.G.
3. Lauryn Hill
4. Jay-Z
5. Nas

6. Kendrick Lamar
7. J. Cole
8. Nicki Minaj
9. Cardi B
10. Drake

Some Common Core ELA/Literacy Standards Reflected in this Assignment

CCSS.ELA-LITERACY.CCRA.R.2
CCSS.ELA-LITERACY.CCRA.R.3
CCSS.ELA-LITERACY.CCRA.R.5
CCSS.ELA-LITERACY.CCRA.R.6
CCSS.ELA-LITERACY.CCRA.R.7
CCSS.ELA-LITERACY.CCRA.R.9
CCSS.ELA-LITERACY.CCRA.W.1
CCSS.ELA-LITERACY.CCRA.W.2
CCSS.ELA-LITERACY.CCRA.W.7
CCSS.ELA-LITERACY.CCRA.W.8
CCSS.ELA-LITERACY.CCRA.W.9
CCSS.ELA-LITERACY.CCRA.SL.3
CCSS.ELA-LITERACY.CCRA.SL.4
CCSS.ELA-LITERACY.CCRA.SL.5

Assignment Five: Hip Hop Autobiography

At some point in their secondary school experiences, most students are asked to write a version of a memoir or personal narrative. This assignment encourages students to reflect on their stories and identities, including some of the transformative moments in their lives that shaped who they are and how they see the world. In my English classes, students were most challenged by the exercise of recalling and choosing these moments. By adolescence, young people have collected an abundance of memories, and choosing just one or a few of these to encapsulate their personhood can be overwhelming. Similar to the "Class Playlist" activity described in Lesson Two, this assignment helps to narrow students' focus in order to facilitate meaningful reflections about their lives and identities through the writing of a Hip Hop Autobiography.

The Hip Hop Autobiography is similar to a written memoir or personal narrative except that it asks students to tell the story of their engagement with Hip Hop music and culture. Because Hip Hop culture is a predominant force in youth culture at the same time that young people's engagement with Hip Hop is diverse and unique to their individual identities, this assignment works to tease out the intersections between students' identities and their interaction with popular culture, including their understandings of how factors such as race, class, gender, and sexuality have impacted their lives and the construction of their identities. This assignment can take the form of a written narrative, a video, a song or music album, or another creative approach to storytelling.

While most of my students chose to submit a written narrative, one student created a spoken word poetry EP accompanied by an artist's statement summarizing how the poems fit together to tell the story of her development through Hip Hop culture, communities, and sensibilities. Unlike class assignments that focused on textual analysis, the autobiography provided an opportunity for the students to explicitly reflect on their personal stories and to consider how their engagement with popular media influenced their identities. Whereas class discussion highlighted *what* as well as *how* my students thought, their written narratives showed me the roots of these ideologies. Thus, the Hip Hop autobiographies served as an integral puzzle piece in my own understanding of my students.

A running joke in my class one year was that one of the students, Drew, consistently listened to music that other students saw as silly or superficial in comparison to the lyrically dense songs that otherwise dominated class discourse. When sharing this music in class, Drew's explanations were a variation of "I just like it." However, Drew's Hip Hop autobiography told a more specific story. According to his narrative, Drew gravitated towards this type of music because it was a reminder to him that someone who was not born into a life of privilege could still find success even if they are not considered a "Black Savant" (Bhabha,

2004) or member of the "Talented Tenth" (Du Bois, 1903). The popularity of these artists gave Drew hope that he, too, could "make it" in society. Reading Drew's Hip Hop autobiography reframed how I understood him, his engagement in class, and his connections to Hip Hop music. Not only did this assignment provide me with insights through which I could better teach my students, but it also provided students such as Drew with a language and vehicle for expressing their current realities and their visions for their future.

Sample Directions for Students

An autobiography is the chronological story of an individual's journey. As a final assessment for the class, you will write or create your Hip Hop autobiography that describes your individual development through or with Hip Hop. This piece can take the form of writing, a short film, an EP (a mini album), or a pre-approved alternate medium. Your autobiography should answer the following questions:

♦ What role does Hip Hop play in your life?
♦ When did Hip Hop come into your life?
♦ What parts of Hip Hop do you most connect with? (i.e., language, fashion, music, art, history, themes, etc.)
♦ What specific people or artifacts were instrumental in your development? (i.e., seeing Jay live in concert; getting a mixtape from my best friend; hearing *Illmatic* for the first time, etc.)
♦ In what way or where do you see yourself in Hip Hop?
♦ How has Hip Hop contributed to your development as an individual?

Assignment Variations

Hanif Abdurraqib's (2019) book of personal essays, *Go Ahead in the Rain: Notes to A Tribe Called Quest* is essentially a memoir told through his reflections on the indelible rap group A Tribe Called Quest. Using Abdurraqib's writing as a mentor text, students can write a memoir or personal narrative through the lens of a particular artist, group, song, or album. In this variation of the Hip Hop Autobiography, rather than focus on their engagement with Hip Hop, the students use their reflections on the chosen artist(s) or piece of art as a touchpoint to develop a narrative of significant moments in their lives or of the development of their worldviews.

Some Common Core ELA/Literacy Standards Reflected in this Assignment

CCSS.ELA-LITERACY.CCRA.W.2
CCSS.ELA-LITERACY.CCRA.W.3
CCSS.ELA-LITERACY.CCRA.W.4
CCSS.ELA-LITERACY.W.9–10.2.A
CCSS.ELA-LITERACY.W.9–10.2.B
CCSS.ELA-LITERACY.W.9–10.2.C
CCSS.ELA-LITERACY.W.9–10.2.D
CCSS.ELA-LITERACY.W.9–10.3.A
CCSS.ELA-LITERACY.W.9–10.3.B
CCSS.ELA-LITERACY.W.9–10.3.C
CCSS.ELA-LITERACY.W.9–10.3.D
CCSS.ELA-LITERACY.W.9–10.3.E

Note

1   A Google search of each of these artists with the term "real" or "fake" brings up a plethora of articles about plastic surgery but very little about their lyrics or lives.

4

Teaching Hip Hop as a Content Area

So far in this book, we have explored ways to incorporate popular texts, in particular Hip Hop texts, into existing curriculum and instruction. It is also important to recognize, however, the need to develop courses that explicitly teach with and about Hip Hop. As a form of history, culture, and literature that directly impacts the lives, identities, and even futures of our students, Hip Hop warrants its own course of study beyond individual Hip Hop-focused units or lessons. In fact, Hip Hop is a rapidly growing field of study across the U.S. and globally, with entire courses, programs, and degrees dedicated to Hip Hop studies in colleges and universities, including Columbia University, Harvard University, Rutgers University, Howard University, the University of California, Los Angeles, Wellesley College, Columbia College, Bowie State University, New York University, the University of Missouri, the University of Arizona, and Indiana University, to name a few. Along with this rise in Hip Hop studies, Hip Hop archives and research centers have been developed at institutions such as Cornell University, Harvard University, the University of Washington, and the University of Massachusetts, Boston. These sites represent a growing scholarly and curatorial interest in preserving and cataloging the rich history of Hip Hop culture.

DOI: 10.4324/9781003293767-4

As research on ethnic studies has made clear (de los Ríos, 2020), developing courses dedicated to the study of historically marginalized communities and cultures is necessary in the effort to close the "opportunity gap" (Carter & Welner, 2013) or the "education debt" (Ladson-Billings, 2006) owed to students of color in U.S. schools. Ensuring that these students' communities and histories are centered in the curriculum, rather than relegated to holidays, footnotes, or bonus materials, goes a long way towards disrupting the dominant curriculum that has consistently ignored the needs and identities of minoritized communities.

In contrast to an often-held belief that Hip Hop is a musical genre that promotes hypersexuality and materialism (Rose, 2008), Hip Hop, in actuality, represents a form of art, community, and culture for those who identify with its elements. Additionally, understanding the history and culture of Hip Hop is, at this point, critical to understanding Black American history and modern youth culture. Recognizing the significance of Hip Hop in academic spaces can reinforce to students the integral contributions that Black and Latinx communities, including youth communities, have made to the history and culture of the U.S., a contribution that is often invisiblized in schools and in media. Hill (2009), for example, described how the students in the school where he taught a Hip Hop Literature class naturally perceived the class as a "Black space":

> Despite the racial diversity of the classroom, students of all races frequently referred to Hip-Hop Lit as the "Black people class" or, among the Black students, simply "our class." While alternately playful and serious, these comments indexed the ways in which Hip-Hop Lit was imagined and discussed within the community as a Black space.
>
> (p. 49)

Hill's observation highlights the fact that in contrast to the Eurocentric curriculum that permeates most K-12 school classrooms, Hip Hop courses can present to students one of few, if not the only, academic spaces that center Blackness. I encountered a similar phenomenon during the first week that I taught a college Hip Hop literature course. After class, one of my students, a young Black woman, approached me to thank me for teaching the course, stating, "We've never had a Black studies class here before." I was caught off guard by this comment. While I had thought of the class as a literature course that happened to focus on Hip Hop, for this student, and perhaps for many others, it represented something much more— it was an opportunity to learn and think about Blackness from a more expansive framework than those that are typically provided to students.

In addition to providing a powerful content area for teaching students of color and urban youth, Hip Hop also offers a site for the sociopolitical development of all students, including youth and adults from more dominant or privileged backgrounds who can benefit from exposure to asset-based perspectives on Black and Latinx culture that complicate the singular narratives of slavery, migration, and civil rights that often comprise dominant approaches to these histories. Having taught Hip Hop courses in suburban and racially diverse classrooms, I can attest to the power of Hip Hop studies in cultivating students' racial literacies (Sealey-Ruiz, 2013) as well as fostering their recognition of the scientific, linguistic, literary, mathematical, and technological contributions of Hip Hop innovators to American life.

Teaching Hip Hop literature and culture courses in secondary and undergraduate schools has revealed to me both the urgency and impact of introducing Hip Hop studies into academic spaces as well as the particularities involved in doing this work within school structures that were not designed for such transformative teaching and learning, especially involving popular music and culture. Based on my experiences in teaching Hip Hop literature and culture courses, I offer the following suggestions and guidelines for teachers preparing to teach Hip Hop as a content area.

"Move B!$*%; Get Out the Way!": Decentering the Self in Hip Hop Curriculum and Pedagogy

A concern that many pre-service and in-service teachers often raise is that they do not feel confident enough in their knowledge and understanding of Hip Hop to introduce it into the classroom. Indeed, those who elect to teach Hip Hop courses are often "Hip Hop heads" who are excited to share their Hip Hop-based knowledge, experiences, and passions with their students. Admittedly, I started out as one of those teachers. Even before meeting my students, I had designed the entire curriculum, complete with Essential Questions, formative and summative assignments, and core texts, primarily made up of the lyrics to Hip Hop songs that reflected the themes of each unit. I was *thrilled* about my curriculum and the prospect of studying these classic and seminal Hip Hop songs and documentaries with students in a classroom setting.

Thus, instead of viewing the class as a collaboration with my students, I had treated it like most traditional approaches to school curriculum, predetermining what was important knowledge for my students rather than starting with what they already knew and cared about. Based on my own Hip Hop identities, I had essentially designed the class that my teenage self would have wanted to be in rather than creating the class that my students needed. I came to this realization after processing the results of the first class assessment—a quiz on Hip Hop history.

The first unit of the class provided an overview of Hip Hop history and included such foundational songs as "The Message" by Grandmaster Flash and the Furious Five and "Rapper's Delight," by the Sugarhill Gang. We also watched Charlie Ahearn's 1983 film *Wild Style* in addition to videos documenting the early years of Hip Hop and read excerpts from Jeff Chang's (2005) *Can't Stop Won't Stop: A History of the Hip Hop Generation*. When I created the end of unit quiz, I was genuinely excited for my students, thinking, "I would have LOVED to take a Hip Hop history quiz in high school." The quiz included questions such as "What DJ is credited with starting Rap?" (DJ Kool Herc) and "Who invented the Quick Mix theory of cutting, the backspin, and the double-back?" (Grandmaster Flash). When the majority of my students received scores of 65 and under on this quiz, I first became frustrated that the students hadn't "paid attention." And then, I let go of my ego and confronted the fact that the problem wasn't the students but rather my curriculum. Figure 4.1 shows one of

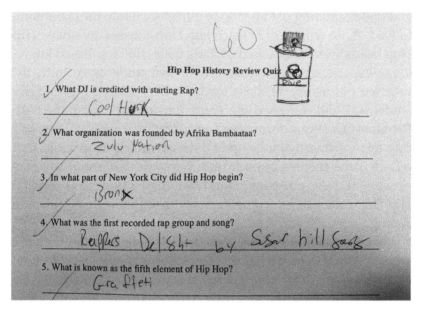

FIGURE 4.1 Student's Hip Hop History Quiz

the students' completed quizzes from this unit. This student's impromptu drawing of a graffiti spray paint can on the top of his quiz is more reflective of his familiarity with Hip Hop culture than answers to a quiz can be.

As I recalled the lessons that led up to this end-of-unit assessment, I reckoned with the fact that my students had seemed a bit disconnected from the material. They weren't particularly excited to watch the films or to read whole chapters about Hip Hop's history. In fact, they responded to these early lessons in much the same way that high school students might respond to any history class. While the details of Hip Hop's birth and development are certainly important to understanding the significance of Hip Hop, they were not of particular importance to my students at that point in time. In assessing my approach to this class, I realized that I had done the same thing with Hip Hop that teachers do with any content area in which they consider themselves experts, determining what knowledge is significant without direct input from students. As teachers, we need to be mindful of how we might inadvertently wield our love or knowledge of Hip Hop over our students, creating a Hip Hop canon and schoolifying a culture and art form through tests and finite answers.

In spite of its universal appeal, Hip Hop is very much context specific and must be taught as such. I consequently revised my curriculum, removing most of the pre-selected texts and, instead, focusing on the Essential Questions, inviting students to choose the songs that they felt best reflected these questions. Thus, the seminal texts in our class were not by KRS-One, Nas, or Jay-Z; rather, our class discussions dealt with how ideas regarding race, class, gender, and power were reflected in the work of 2 Chainz, Drake, and Nicki Minaj. Ultimately, students' engagement and critical development in this Hip Hop class increased the more I got out of the way.

Perhaps it is the case that those who have less knowledge and experience of youth popular culture might be best positioned to work with Hip Hop in the classroom as the lack of Hip Hop-based background essentially forces teachers to be students, learning with and from their students. In fact, those who enter Hip Hop-based classes rooted only in their own personal experiences with Hip Hop rather than those of students may run the risk of establishing or maintaining classroom hierarchies and further distancing students from engagement in school. If Hip Hop pedagogy is to disrupt the status quo of structural hierarchies and institutional oppression, then it requires that teachers be willing to disrupt their own institutionalization, inviting students to be co-teachers and co-creators of curriculum that draws from and impacts their lives.

"Tear the Roof Off!": Reframing Teaching Through a Hip Hop Lens

As is made evident in the earlier example, teaching with and about Hip Hop requires both a decentering of teacher knowledge and identity as well as a decentering or disruption of traditional schooling structures. Unlike dominant approaches to classroom teaching, Hip Hop pedagogy cannot be distilled into a literary canon or the memorization of dates, facts, people, locations, and equations. These practices are arguably antithetical to the ethos of Hip Hop itself, which is, by nature, fluid, disruptive, and co-constructed.

In order to engage with Hip Hop not only as a form of history, literature, or art but also as a way of being, educators must reflect Hip Hop-based practices in their design of Hip Hop coursework. This includes modeling classes after a cypher, a Hip Hop practice in which individuals gather in some form of a circle and take turns performing and practicing their skills; striving for the development of self-knowledge, Hip Hop's fifth and most crucial element; engaging in collaboration, a merging of students' individual skills and talents to create something representative of the collective; and resisting oppression by challenging structures that reinforce inequities, especially those that disproportionately impact the most vulnerable individuals and communities in our society. Through this lens, teachers should be tapping into Hip Hop cultural knowledge and practice in order to transform school spaces rather than using elements of Hip Hop to uphold schooling structures that have historically underserved and, let's be honest, traumatized those who have been marginalized based on race, class, gender, sexuality, ability, language, citizenship status, or an intersection of these.

In a class that engages authentically with the core values of Hip Hop culture, teachers should be prepared to ask such critical questions as these: Are tests and quizzes the most appropriate way to assess student learning in this class? What does it mean and look like to show proficiency in Hip Hop Education? What are my goals for students in this class, and do my goals align with those of my students? How does this class reflect, challenge, or otherwise engage with the dominant views on schooling that are reflected in Hip Hop music and culture? In what ways do my students have voice and agency in this class? How are students invited to provide feedback on my curriculum and teaching and/ or participate in these processes? How does this class engage with communities beyond the classroom walls?

As mentioned previously, these guidelines come from my own learning as I navigated teaching my first Hip Hop Literature and Culture class. In particular, I entered the class with the assumption that changing the *content* of my teaching without changing my actual practices would be sufficient in disrupting traditional approaches to classroom pedagogy. In addition to the unsuccessful Hip Hop history quiz, another indicator that my pedagogy needed to shift was my students' response to the class study guides. As I mentioned earlier, the class studied documentary videos and scholarly writing in addition to song lyrics. To support my students' study of these texts, I distributed study guides such as those shared in *Appendix C*. These handouts were collected for homework and classwork grades. Although the students were engaged in class discussion of these texts, many had low grades for the course as a result of not completing the study guides or forgetting to hand them in. Seeing my students' grades in this class caused me to reflect on many of the questions listed previously. *What does it mean*, I wondered, *for students who identify with, engage with, and practice Hip Hop outside of school to fail a Hip Hop class?* Again, the issue lay not with the students but rather with how I was choosing to assess student learning.

When I met with some of these students for what Professor Christopher Emdin refers to as a "co-gen," a co-generative dialogue regarding how these students were experiencing the class and how their experiences could be improved (Emdin, 2016), the first thing that Drew stated was, "Less questions on those packets!" He said it as though he had been holding on to this thought for weeks and was relieved to finally share it. According to Drew, the study guides were arduous to complete and stressful. What Drew's critique highlights is not that study guides are problematic, as these can be extremely helpful in students' notetaking, processing, and preparing for class discussion, but rather that the requirement for students to complete and submit these study guides as a form of assessment is limiting. For as much as I had been socialized as a teacher to assess students through measures such as these, Drew had been socialized to perform at a certain level on these measures in order to succeed in school. As a result, Drew felt anxious regarding his work for class since the handouts "counted" toward his grade.

The lesson here is that changing the content of instruction is not enough if the approach to instruction does not also change.

When I realized this, I began to shift my approach to class assessments to be more student-driven and presentation-based, gauging learning as well as my teaching in ways that were more organic to the students and to the culture of Hip Hop. This also meant that I shifted my attention away from students' learning about Hip Hop history and culture and toward students' self-reflections and critical analysis of their own popular media engagement. It is *this* approach that became transformative for student learning in this class since these skills challenged students to critically interrogate themselves and their social world in ways that previous classes had not.

Figures 4.2, 4.3, and 4.4 highlight the themes that can arise when classroom study of Hip Hop is student-led and student-centered. Figures 4.2 and 4.3 are photos of an activity facilitated by a group of students in my Hip Hop literature class. By researching the educational histories of successful rappers alongside famous politicians and entrepreneurs, these students facilitated a powerful classroom dialogue that examined the intersections of race, schooling, and future outcomes. Figure 4.4 depicts discussion questions developed by a group of students in the Hip Hop literature class who facilitated a necessary dialogue about Hip Hop and mental health. In both of these student facilitations, Hip Hop became a lens by which the students

FIGURE 4.2 Student-Led Activity Attributing Quotes about Education to Politicians or Rappers

FIGURE 4.3 Student-Led Activity Comparing College Graduation Facts Alongside KRS-One Quote about Knowledge and Intelligence

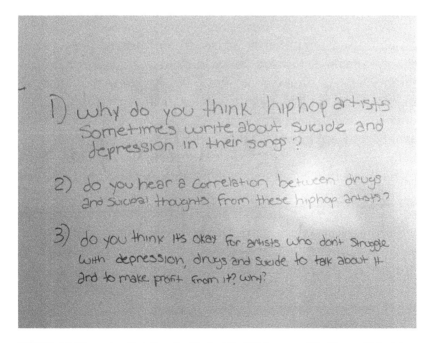

FIGURE 4.4 Discussion Questions for Student-Led Dialogue on Hip Hop and Mental Health

analyzed complex concepts and institutions that are consequential for their lives both individually and collectively.

"If You Stay Ready": Demonstrating Flexibility and Responsiveness in Hip Hop Education

For teachers, knowing and routinizing our curriculum is often a key component in feeling that we have "mastered" our craft. Yet, the fluid nature of popular culture means that knowledge and expertise in this field are constantly shifting. As a result, Hip Hop educators cannot maintain a curriculum that is static and unchanging at the same time that youth culture and students' realities remain in flux. It is here that Hip Hop curriculum diverges most drastically from traditional curriculum since its content is created and recreated every day. While this idea might appear daunting to many teachers, we must recall that if the goal of Hip Hop pedagogy is to acknowledge and be responsive to students' lives, then we must be prepared to shift our plans in response to what is occurring outside of the classroom.

In fact, in Charlotte Danielson's (2008) *Framework for Teaching*, a guide used ubiquitously across school districts and universities, Domain 3, focused on Instruction, emphasizes the need for teachers to demonstrate flexibility and responsiveness in their instruction by making adjustments when necessary, seizing opportunities "to enhance learning, building on a spontaneous event or student interests" (p. 92). Hip Hop pedagogy lends itself to this instructional practice since it demands that teachers adjust plans frequently based on students' interests and needs as well as significant occurrences in the popular culture and media landscape. This approach does not mean that we enter our classrooms without lesson plans or structure; rather, we must be ready and willing to "freestyle" some lessons or quickly remix them in order to remain relevant for students.

An example of this freestyling occurred one semester when I was teaching a Hip Hop Literature course. Over the weekend, rapper Remy Ma released the song "ShEther," a diss track aimed at rapper Nicki Minaj and rhymed over the instrumental from

Nas's classic diss track towards Jay-Z, "Ether." Diss tracks are a common occurrence in rap and would ordinarily not have been of significant note in our class were it not for the fact that this track was FIRE; was more direct and explicit than most in naming and describing the target of the song; was uncharacteristically lengthy at over 7 minutes long; and made appropriate use of an instrumental track, produced by Ron Browz, which is associated with one of the greatest diss tracks ever in Hip Hop.

Although I had already planned a specific lesson for the class, I realized that we could not possibly move forward without addressing the implications of "ShEther." This freestyled lesson involved first listening to the track as a class for those who had not heard it yet, then examining the lyrics to make sense of and discuss both the dense content and the literary artistry. Finally, we engaged in a whole class dialogue about the implications of this song, including its significance in the ongoing dialogue regarding women and feminism in Hip Hop music and culture. As much as the idea of freestyling or quickly remixing lesson plans might seem at odds with teacher training and practice, it reflects the ideas of culturally relevant pedagogy (Ladson-Billings, 1995), an approach that is promoted by most teacher education programs. This approach to Hip Hop coursework also reinforces the need to

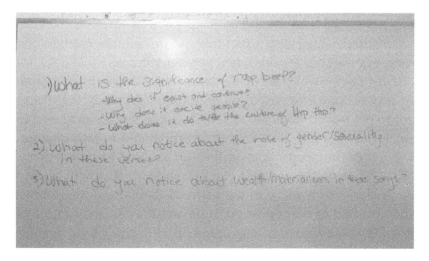

FIGURE 4.5 Discussion Questions for Impromptu Lesson on "ShEther"

collaborate with students in classroom teaching and curriculum since students might have even more expertise to contribute to some lessons than their teachers do.

In order to create a Hip Hop-based classroom that is flexible and responsive, teachers can establish specific daily or weekly structures that guide classroom procedures and student participation. For example, the first few minutes of Monday's class each week might be spent sharing Hip Hop-based news. Perhaps there is a section of Friday's class entitled "Freestyle Fridays" in which students either freestyle or share their favorite rap freestyle verses with the class. Structures such as these can establish class routines while accounting for the dynamic nature of popular culture. These structures can also help students prepare for their own contributions to the class.

In addition to weekly structures, there should also be procedures for responding to texts such that regardless of what material is the focus of class discussion, students know the established protocols for engaging with the texts in the classroom space. In my Hip Hop Literature classes, we established a procedure in which students who were sharing or presenting a song would play the audio of the song while simultaneously displaying and scrolling through the song's lyrics in real-time. This was how we listened to Remy Ma's "ShEther" and subsequently engaged in whole-class dialogue based on the established procedures for class discussion.

By establishing clear structures and procedures, teachers can re-mix or freestyle lessons when necessary in a way that does not disrupt the flow of class or the teacher's ability to be prepared. As rapper Suga Free stated, as long as one stays ready, they "ain't got to get ready" (Blake et al., 1997). If teachers are prepared to work with popular texts in the classroom and to facilitate dialogue regarding popular texts, they do not need to adhere themselves to static lessons and curriculum since they will always be prepared to work with the material that is most relevant to students and to the course goals on any day. As an example of this, *Appendix D* shares a sample Hip Hop studies curriculum presented through Essential Questions rather than through predetermined texts and assignments.

"Teach Me How to Dougie": Modeling Critical Media Literacies and Discussion in the Classroom

Another consideration for teaching Hip Hop in traditional school environments is the possibility that students may not be prepared to engage with transformative approaches to teaching and learning. This can occur for a multitude of reasons, the primary one of which is the years of experience that students have already had with traditional curriculum and pedagogy in K-12 classrooms. After being told implicitly and explicitly that their primary responsibility in school is to listen and absorb information, students become accustomed to the structure of teacher as expert and student as learner, often taking comfort in the clarity and predictability of these roles.

In my high school Hip Hop class, I found that my students had experienced so many years of training within traditional classrooms that they had developed strategies for navigating school structures that did not translate into our class. Drew, for example, as discussed earlier, relied on his ability to complete class handouts in order to succeed in class. The class requirements to give presentations and participate in discussions were new and daunting for many of the students who were accustomed to flying under the radar and sitting in neat, structured rows, ready to jot down and submit the required information. I realized that I was expecting my students to engage in class in entirely new ways than they had in previous classes that were not deeply connected to their identities and to youth popular culture. As a result, these students weren't exactly sure how to engage with this class, including how to facilitate or participate in discussions of the media that they consumed regularly.

To address this challenge, I began to model for the students how to develop critical media literacy practices, including asking questions of texts, noticing language and details, and making connections across texts. When students presented songs to the class, I kicked off the discussion of the songs by displaying these practices and noticed that slowly the other students would start to join in the dialogue, answering questions that I had asked or contributing additional questions and insights. I also modeled presenting songs to the class, providing focal points before sharing the song and offering discussion questions afterward to begin the dialogue. When I played films for the class, I modeled note-taking and returning to my notes during class discussions. Over time, these practices became normalized in the classroom, such that most of the students readily participated in dialogue, used notes in class discussion, presented songs to the class with specific questions and foci, and encouraged each other to be thoughtful and self-reflective in their responses to texts and to each other. An example of this can be seen in the dialogue that follows, excerpted from a high school Hip Hop Literature and Culture class discussion of the songs, "Ridin'" by Chamillionaire and "Locked Up" by Akon, featuring Styles P. In this discussion, I served as facilitator (LLK), posing questions about the texts while the students worked together to examine the texts for their significance to the students' realities.

Sasha: That was so good.

LLK: What did we see? What did we get from it?

Jake: He didn't want to be in jail. And . . .

Leon: They regretted their actions.

LLK: Say that again. Where did you see the regret?

Jake: When they were like, "I got a family that loves me and wants me to do right."

Sasha: Yeah, that's where it was.

Mark: But they stopped visiting him.

LLK: Say that again?

Mark: He said they stopped visiting him in jail.

LLK: Oh, I missed that part. I didn't see that. Did it seem like he was this, like, "criminal" who hurt people and . . .

Jake: Well Styles P did.

LLK: There was the part where Styles P was like, "I might go back again." Right? And he was also talking about "murking people," which means . . .

Jake: Killing

LLK: Killing people . . . but Akon's character at one point said something like, "I'm steady trying to find a motive for why I do what I do." Can anyone make sense of that?

Jake: He like keeps trying to find a reason for why he does bad things.

LLK: Do you know people like that?

Multiple: Yeah.

LLK: *Is* there a motive? Like, are some people just, like naturally—do they just do bad things?

Anthony: Search your identity.

Jake: Well at the time doing what they did made sense to them. Then . . .

LLK: Until they got caught and then they were like, "Hmm . . . that was a mistake?"

Jake: Well not even until they got caught. Until like after when they realized it was wrong.

LLK: Interesting.

Sasha: I don't really think it's malicious. Like a lot of people when they're, like—desperate times call for desperate measures. Y'know?

LLK: Hmmm. Say more about that.

Sasha: Like, a lot of times if someone's poor and the only thing that they can do is like sell drugs and then they get into jail for that. It's like, "I had to feed my family."

In this excerpt, we can see the students quickly responding to the prompts with evidence from the text and with their own understandings of the world. The students also demonstrate ease and comfort in this dialogue, sharing their ideas without pressure to have a "correct" answer or say the "right" thing. There is also a moment in the dialogue where Mark points out a line in the song that I hadn't previously noticed, demonstrating how meaning is co-constructed in Hip Hop literacy dialogue and highlighting how teachers can facilitate students' learning without being experts on the class material. It is critical to note that this dialogue occurred in the middle of the semester, after weeks of having modeled critical media literacies for my students. The discussions early in the semester were quite different from the one seen here, with large spaces of silence and students uncertainly responding more out of obligation than enthusiasm. Thus, I reiterate how important it is for teachers to have patience with

themselves and with their students as they work together to dismantle hierarchical and long-standing classroom practices that
decenter student knowledge and to work towards building a
participatory, youth-led, dialogic classroom environment that
engages critically with popular media and culture.

"For My People": Engaging with Hip Hop Community

As discussed previously, a core feature of Hip Hop culture is that
of community. Anyone who has read a book, watched a documentary, or listened to a podcast on Hip Hop history can attest
to this since the most significant stories that are told of this culture almost always involve communal events. Some of these
include DJ Kool Herc and his sister Cindy Campbell's "Back
to School Jam" in 1973, an event which established Herc as the
"Father" of Hip Hop sound; the proliferation of Hip Hop block
parties across New York City, particularly in the Bronx; and a
multitude of concerts and gatherings through which DJ's, pro-
ducers, rappers, singers, graffiti writers, and breakers met and
collaborated. Popular podcasts such as "The People's Party,"
"Drink Champs," and "The Breakfast Club" are centered on such
pivotal moments in Hip Hop history, exemplifying the reality
that without community, there is no Hip Hop.

Earlier in this book, we discussed the importance of building
community within classrooms as a way to support students'
academic, critical, social, and emotional development. Within
a Hip Hop class, developing a classroom community is just
as important, if not more so, since students are more directly
responsible for contributing to the structures and content of a
Hip Hop class. However, in classes dedicated to the study of Hip
Hop, community-building involves much more than connecting
to other students in the class. In order to tap into all that Hip Hop
offers as a site for historical, cultural, critical, social, academic,
and activist development, students in Hip Hop-based classes
must be connected to the larger Hip Hop community outside of
the classroom. This community-building can take many forms,
including connecting with Hip Hop-based organizations such as
those listed in *Appendix E* or creating an event in the school or

community that celebrates Hip Hop and invites those from out-side of the Hip Hop class to participate.

Weeks into the semester of the first Hip Hop Literature and Culture course that I taught, it occurred to me that I had overlooked a crucial component in planning for class. We had been discussing Hip Hop for weeks and yet had not actively engaged in any of its elements aside from that of knowledge. This felt like a critical oversight. However, I was also self-aware enough to know that I lacked the skills to adequately perform or teach all four of Hip Hop's artistic elements to my students. In my quest to find teaching artists who could visit my classroom and work with the students, I had a pivotal conversation with Dr. Ernest Morrell, my mentor and one of the earliest scholars of Hip Hop Education. Dr. Morrell offered the idea that it might be more fruitful to bring the teaching artists together to meet and work with the students for a single day. This would also allow for students from other schools and organizations to attend and build community with one another.

We subsequently organized a one-day Hip Hop youth summit that brought together high school and college students from across the city who were all in some way students and/or practitioners in the field of Hip Hop, spoken word poetry, and social justice education. During this day, students engaged in workshops facilitated by Hip Hop artist-educators, student presentations, a talk by Dr. Christopher Emdin, and a youth-led dialogue about students' experiences in schools. Throughout the day, I witnessed my students interacting in ways that were dis-tinct from when we were in class together, spurred on by the skillful facilitation of the workshop presenters and the oppor-tunity to build authentic relationships with other young people who share similar identities. As we left the event, my students were overflowing with excitement about what they experienced that day. Drew, for example, expressed his surprise and joyful wonder that he had met a professor who spoke the same way that he did and who "liked Hip Hop the way I like Hip Hop." In fact, this is a sentiment that I often hear expressed by youth who encounter teachers and professors in Hip Hop spaces. For young people enculturated into mainstream schooling practices, encountering adults who have successfully combined their love for Hip Hop with their professional lives, especially in academic spaces, provides new lenses for them to think about their own complex identities and their visions for the future. On the way home from the summit, another student shared:

> Today was, like, a life-changing experience. It helped me, like, on my journey to what I want to do in life, and it was seriously, like, the best day of my life. . ... The things that I learned—speaking to real human beings. I've never had an interaction with a person where I felt such warmth and I felt a connection.

As these students' testimonials exemplify, engaging with Hip Hop community is a powerful way for students to feel seen, to move towards self-actualization, or Knowledge of Self, and to begin to envision futures for themselves that encompass the fullness of their identities. Next I offer suggestions for fostering students' engagement with Hip Hop-based communities outside of the classroom.

FIGURE 4.6 Students Working on a Chalkboard Graffiti Mural at the Hip Hop Youth Summit

Field Trips

As Hip Hop increasingly becomes recognized as a foundational element in U.S. history and society, there has been a significant rise in the number of museums and institutions displaying Hip Hop-based exhibits that teachers can visit with their students. The idea that institutions such as The Smithsonian Museum in Washington, D.C., carry artifacts documenting Hip Hop history and culture is a powerful reminder to students that their cultures and histories are valued and should be honored as well as preserved. *Appendix F* contains a list of museums that teachers might consider visiting with their students. In addition to these permanent collections, there are also Hip Hop-based exhibitions available to visit at museums and art spaces across the U.S. and across the world. Teachers should also consider visiting local landmarks in their communities that display elements of Hip Hop culture. Figure 4.7, for example, captures a powerful moment for the students in my Hip Hop Literature and Culture

FIGURE 4.7 Hip Hop Literature and Culture Class Trip to View Graffiti Murals at 5 Pointz in Queens, New York

class when we visited 5 Pointz, a bastion of graffiti art and community in New York City, shortly before its demolition in 2013.

Conferences

There are several Hip Hop-focused conferences designed to bring together youth, educators, community members, artists, and activists for presentations, dialogues, and workshops focused on Hip Hop culture (See *Appendix E*). As reflected in my description of the Hip Hop Youth Summit, such events can reframe how students see themselves as well as how they view the roles of education and community in their individual growth and in the development of their futures. The Hip Hop Ex Lab's "Can't Stop Hip Hop" conference and the Hip Hop Youth Research and Activism conference are two examples of intergenerational spaces that invite youth to teach, learn, perform, and participate in the co-construction of Hip Hop culture and community.

Guest Speakers and Teaching Artists

Whether or not teachers have access to the time, resources, or permissions necessary to bring students on a field trip or to a conference, it is also fruitful to connect students to Hip Hop community members by inviting guest speakers or teaching artists to the school to give a presentation or teach a workshop either in the classroom or to a larger audience beyond the classroom. This presentation can introduce students to professionals from outside of the school who engage in Hip Hop practices, such as b-boying/b-girling, DJing, producing, emceeing, archiving, curating, film-directing, and teaching. This can also help to decenter the teacher as the sole adult or expert in the classroom, showing the students that their teacher also works in collaboration with others and does not see themselves as the crux of their students' learning.

Teachers inviting guests into the classroom should be mindful of the need to compensate these guests for their time and expertise. Oftentimes, the services that Hip Hop artists and educators provide are undervalued, and these professionals are underpaid or not paid at all. If the school does not have funds for an honorarium for guests, consider a class fundraiser, organizing

FIGURE 4.8 Youth Leaders Facilitating a Workshop on Hip Hop and Self-Love at the Annual Hip Hop Youth Research and Activism Conference

an evening talk or performance featuring this guest and in which proceeds can go towards their honorarium, or offering a meaningful "Thank You" gift that has value for the guest presenter. Guests can also be invited to join the class virtually, which may draw less upon their time and negates the need for funds associated with travel and accommodations.

Social Media

In addition to providing in-person experiences, teachers can also expose their students to Hip Hop communities through social media. Forums such as Clubhouse, Instagram Live, and Twitter provide real-time opportunities for students to engage with practitioners of Hip Hop arts, education, and activism, sharing their ideas and experiences as well as learning from and with others outside of their classroom or school community. The #hiphoped Twitter chat, which occurs weekly on Tuesdays, is one example of an intergenerational, digital space that builds community across geographic locations and promotes critical discussion of Hip Hop as it lives in schools and in society. Since our youth now live in an irreversibly digital world, connecting students to digital Hip Hop communities is a culturally relevant and accessible way to support their development and their building of expansive, intergenerational communities.

5

Closing Thoughts

This book intentionally centers Hip Hop music and culture in its offerings and many of the strategies shared herein are specific to this form of pedagogy. However, it is also important to note that the strategies shared apply not only to Hip Hop-based courses but also to any class dedicated to culturally relevant pedagogy and to the study of youth culture and popular texts, including, for example, comics and films.

Additionally, as much as the aforementioned guidelines are offered to support teachers' development of Hip Hop-based classrooms and communities, there truly is no way to predict or fully preempt all that may come with engaging directly with youth identities and popular culture in the classroom. There is no singular or correct way of doing this work since every teacher, student, and classroom carries their own stories and needs. We also live in a time in which technological advancements and media output occur so swiftly that the world somehow feels more open, possible, fruitful, and transient all at once.

Since the time that I started working with popular texts in the classroom, I have witnessed the shift from students consuming music on iPods and seeking out radio stations to stay abreast of Hip Hop news to now creating and disseminating music on their smartphones along with the ability to connect with the world instantly through live platforms such as those on Instagram, Facebook, and YouTube. This digital transformation reflects both the unpredictability of youth popular culture and the need to

DOI: 10.4324/9781003293767-5

support young people's critical media literacies as a mechanism for survival and success in an increasingly media-driven world. Ultimately, students who possess the ability to self-reflect and develop Knowledge of Self will be prepared to encounter and perhaps transform their social worlds to be more hopeful, more loving, and more just. It is our responsibility, then, as educators to create sites of learning in our classrooms that move students towards these futures through meaningful encounters with media, culture, and community.

Appendix A: Suggestions for Further Reading

Bradley, A. (2017). *Book of rhymes: The poetics of hip hop*. Basic Books.

Bradley, A., & DuBois, A. (2010). *The anthology of rap*. Yale University Press.

Chang, J. (2005). *Can't stop won't stop: A history of the hip-hop generation*. St. Martin's Press.

Emdin, C. (2016). *For White folks who teach in the hood . . . and the rest of y'all too: Reality pedagogy and urban education*. Beacon Press.

Hill, M. L. (2009). *Beats rhymes & classroom life*. Teachers College Press.

Kitwana, B. (2002). *The hip hop generation: Young blacks and the crisis in African American culture*. Basic Civitas Books.

Richardson, E. (2006). *Hiphop literacies*. Routledge.

Riggs, T. (2018). *St. James encyclopedia of Hip Hop culture*. St. James Press.

Runell, M., & Diaz, M. (2007). *The h2ed guidebook: A sourcebook of inspiration & practical application*. Hip-Hop Association.

Sitomer, A. L., & Cirelli, M. (2004). *Hip-hop poetry and the classics: Connecting our classic curriculum to hip-hop poetry through standards-based language arts instruction*. Milk Mug Pub.

Appendix B: Suggested Texts for Hip Hop-Based Curriculum

Abdurraqib, H. (2019). *Go ahead in the rain: Notes to a tribe called quest*. University of Texas Press.

Chang, J., Davey, D., & Kool, DJ. (2021). *Can't stop won't stop: A hip-hop history* (1st ed. Young adult). Wednesday Books.

Drew, K., & Wortham, J. (2020). *Black futures*. One World.

Dunn, S., McFadyen, S., Wheeler, D., Bascunan, R., & Kabango, S. (2019). *Hip-hop evolution*. Palatin Media; New KSM (Available on DVD and Streaming Services).

Hurt, B. (2006). *Hip-hop: Beyond beats and rhymes*. Media Education Foundation (Available onDVD).

National Museum of African American History and Culture (U.S.) & Smithsonian/Folkways Recordings. (2020). *Smithsonian anthology of hip-hop and rap*. Smithsonian Institution.

Pough, G. D. (2004). *Check it while I wreck it: Black womanhood, hip-hop culture, and the public sphere*. Northeastern University Press.

Rose, T. (2008). *The hip hop wars: What we talk about when we talk about Hip Hop – and why it matters*. Basic Civitas Books.

Semtex, D. J., & Chuck, D. (2018). *Hip hop raised me*. Thames & Hudson.

Spirer, P. (1997). *Rhyme & reason*. Miramax Home Entertainment: Distributed by Buena Vista Home Entertainment (Available on DVD and Streaming Services).

Appendix C: Hip Hop Course Study Guide Examples

Wild Style Study Guide

Wild Style is a 1983 Hip Hop film produced by Charlie Ahearn. It is regarded as the first Hip Hop motion picture. The film featured seminal figures within the given period, such as Fab Five Freddy, Lee Quiñones, Lady Pink, the Rock Steady Crew, The Cold Crush Brothers, Queen Lisa Lee of Zulu Nation, and Flash. The protagonist "Zoro" is played by New York graffiti artist "Lee" George Quiñones. The film title is a reference to a particular graffiti style developed by the early writer Tracy 168, which incorporates the use of complex interwoven and overlapping letters and shapes.

♦ What argument are Raymond (Zoro) and his brother having at the beginning of the film?

♦ Based on the basketball scene, what is the connection between basketball and Hip Hop?

♦ What does the presence of the reporter tell you about the connection between graffiti art and mainstream culture?

♦ Why is Zoro so upset about the presence of the reporter?

♦ Why is money so important in this film?

♦ Why do you think the characters act so casually about almost being held up outside of the club?

♦ What does the party scene with the gallery owner and the money commissioning a painting from Zoro tell you about wealth and power in relation to art and Hip Hop?

♦ How do the four elements of Hip Hop come together in this film?

Can't Stop Won't Stop Chapter 11—"Things Fall Apart"

1. How is South African apartheid connected to the civil rights struggle in the U.S.?

2. How did the elders of the civil rights movement view the Hip Hop generation of the 1980s?

3. What does it mean to "divest"?

4. Who is Nelson Mandela?

5. Who is the "father of Black Consciousness?"

6. How was the anti-apartheid student movement of the 1980s different from the civil rights movement of the 1960s?

7. Describe Black-Jewish relations in the U.S. both before and after 1960.

8. What is "White Flight," and how did it lead to "resegregation"?

9. Jeff Chang writes, "In African American history, time and again . . . people turned to male religious figures to deliver them." How might this idea connect to the popularity of rap in the Black community?

10. What social, cultural, and political elements changed rap in the mid-80s?

Hip Hop and the Justice System

"Ridin'," Chamillionaire

♦ What attitudes towards policing does Chamillionaire express?
♦ How are police and criminals portrayed in this song and video?
♦ Are the attitudes and images from the song consistent with what you see in Hip Hop and/or real life? Explain.

"Lock'd Up," Akon

♦ What attitude does the narrator express about prison?
♦ Does the narrator feel that he is guilty?
♦ Do you empathize with the narrator? Why/why not?
♦ Do the attitudes or ideas in this song reflect what you see in Hip Hop or real life? Explain.

"Gone Till November," Wyclef Jean

♦ Where is the narrator going until November?
♦ What does the narrator mean when he says, "I can't work a 9 to 5"?
♦ Why can't the narrator work a 9 to 5?
♦ Is this narrative similar to other stories or attitudes you have heard in Hip Hop or in life? Explain.

Notes, Comments, Questions, Quotes, Ideas:

Appendix D: Sample Hip Hop Course Curriculum

Unit 1: Hip Hop and Its Roots

Essential Question: What physical and social factors led to the creation of Hip Hop culture?

- ◆ How and why did Hip Hop come about?
- ◆ How did the four elements of DJing, breakdancing, emceeing, and graffiti art come together to form the basis of Hip Hop culture?
- ◆ Who were the leaders and participants in early Hip Hop movements?
- ◆ How did Hip Hop both diffuse and exacerbate violence and tension in communities?
- ◆ How did the community and society respond to the introduction of Hip Hop?

Unit 2: Hip Hop, History, and Culture

Essential Question: How does Hip Hop Music document history and reflect culture?

- ◆ What themes are recurrent in Hip Hop lyrics?
- ◆ How do these themes reflect the Black experience in America?
- ◆ How did these themes change over time?
- ◆ How do the changing themes in Hip Hop reflect societal changes for Black Americans?

- Are the ideas and themes present in Hip Hop lyrics accurate portrayals of Black American culture?
- How is sampling a part of Hip Hop music and American culture?

Unit 3: Gender and Hip Hop

Essential Question: How do representations of gender and sexuality in Hip Hop reflect and influence the role of Black men and women in society?

- How are masculinity and femininity portrayed within Hip Hop?
- How does the portrayal of gender identities in Hip Hop influence society's views on gender?
- What pressures or expectations of masculinity and femininity are expressed in Hip Hop music?
- Why has Rap been a male-dominated industry? In what ways has this shifted over time?
- How have women used Hip Hop to re-frame society's views of womanhood?
- How has Hip Hop culture served to re-imagine or solidify images of Black masculinities and femininities?

Unit 4: Hip Hop and the World

Essential Question: How has Hip Hop changed society?

- How has Hip Hop impacted society nationally and globally?
- What is the current state of Hip Hop music?
- Are there limits to who can be involved in Hip Hop production or consumption?

- ◆ How did the commercialization of Hip Hop music and culture affect the Hip Hop community?
- ◆ In what ways is Hip Hop still relevant or no longer relevant to the Black community?
- ◆ How can Hip Hop be used as a tool of activism?

Appendix E: Hip Hop Education Resources, Conferences, and Organizations

- Can't Stop Hip Hop Conference—Annual intergenerational Hip Hop and education conference organized by the HipHopEx Lab.
  - www.cantstophiphop.org/
- Get Free Hip Hop Civics Education—Multimedia Hip Hop civics curriculum and resources for teaching, building community, and fostering youth activism.
  - http://getfreehiphopcivics.com/
- H2ED (Hip-Hop Education) Center—Organization focusing on expanding the field of Hip Hop Education through research, programming, and the cultivation of scholarship.
  - https://hiphopeducation.com/
- #hiphoped—Educational organization that hosts weekly twitter chats, podcasts, and an annual conference on Hip Hop education.
  - https://hiphoped.com/
- HipHopEx Lab—Intergenerational collaborative arts space exploring the intersections of Hip Hop, art, education, and community.
  - https://hiphop.gse.harvard.edu/hiphopex
- Hip Hop Literacies Conference—Annual conference featuring research, practice, and dialogue exploring Hip Hop as it intersects with language, identity, and power.
  - go.osu.edu/hhlc
- Hip Hop Youth Research and Activism (HHYRA) Conference—Annual youth conference featuring workshops,

performances, and discussions on Hip Hop as a form of art and activism.

♦ https://sites.google.com/view/hhyraconference
♦ Urban Word—Organization fostering youth critical literacy and art through training, community-building, and performance.
  ♦ www.urbanword.org/

Appendix F: Suggested Museum Trips for Exploring Hip Hop History and Culture in the U.S.

Chicago Hip Hop Heritage Museum, Chicago, IL
www.customresourceschicago.com/chicagohiphopheritage
museum

Museum at FIT Hip Hop Style Archive; New York, NY
https://www.fitnyc.edu/museum/exhibitions/hip-hop-style.
php

Museum of Graffiti; Miami, FL
https://museumofgraffiti.com/

Museum of Pop Culture; Seattle, WA
www.mopop.org/

Recording Academy Grammy Museum; Los Angeles, CA
https://grammymuseum.org/

Recording Academy Grammy Museum Experience; Newark, NJ
www.grammymuseumexp.org/

Smithsonian National Museum of African American History and
Culture, Washington, DC
https://nmaahc.si.edu/

Trap Music Museum; Atlanta, GA
https://trapmusicmuseum.me/

Universal Hip Hop Museum; Bronx, NY
https://uhhm.org/

References

Alim, S. (2011). Global ill-literacies: Hip hop cultures, youth identities, and the politics of literacy. *Review of Research in Education, 35*, 120–146.

Appleman, D. (2014). *Critical encounters in secondary English: Teaching literacy theory to adolescents.* Teachers College Press.

Bhabha, H. K. (2004). The black savant and the dark princess. *ESQ: A Journal of the American Renaissance, 50*(1), 137–155.

Blake, D., Walker, D., & Hamm, P. (1997). *If u stay ready.* On Street Gospel Polygram.

Carter, P. L., & Welner, K. G. (Eds.). (2013). *Closing the opportunity gap: What America must do to give every child an even chance.* Oxford University Press.

Collins, P. H. (2009). *Black feminist thought: Knowledge consciousness and the politics of empowerment* (2nd ed.). Routledge.

Danielson, C. (2008). *Electronic forms and rubrics for enhancing professional practice: A framework for teaching.* Association for Supervision and Curriculum Development.

de los Ríos, C. V. (2020). Writing oneself into the curriculum: Photovoice journaling in a secondary ethnic studies course. *Written Communication, 37*(4), 487–511.

Dimitriadis, G. (2009). *Performing identity/performing culture: Hip hop as text, pedagogy, and lived practice* (Vol. 1). Peter Lang.

Du Bois, W. E. B. (1903). The talented tenth. In B. T. Washington (Ed.), *The Negro problem: A series of articles by representative American Negroes of today* (pp. 102–104). James Pott and Company.

Emdin, C. (2016). *For White folks who teach in the hood . . . and the rest of y'all too: Reality pedagogy and urban education.* Beacon Press.

Epps, T., & West, K. (2012). Birthday song. *On based on a T.R.U Story.* Def Jam.

Hobbs, R. (2020). *Mind over media: Propaganda education for a digital age.* WW Norton & Company.

hooks, B. (2001). *All about love: New visions.* Harper Perennial.

HOT 97 NY. (2012, October 23). *Kendrick Lamar says "don't call my album A classic!"*. YouTube. Retrieved September 19, 2022, from www.youtube.com/watch?v=s6Z53NvlsJQ&t=65s

Kellner, D., & Share, J. (2005). Toward critical media literacy: Core concepts, debates, organizations, and policy. *Discourse: Studies in the Cultural Politics of Education, 26*(3), 369–386.

Kellner, D., & Share, J. (2007). Critical media literacy, democracy, and the reconstruction of education. In D. Macedo & S. R. Steinberg (Eds.), *Media literacy: A reader* (pp. 3–23). Peter Lang Publishing.

Kelly, L. L. (2016). "You don't have to claim her": Reconstructing black femininity through critical hip-hop literacy. *Journal of Adolescent & Adult Literacy, 59*(5), 529–538.

Kitwana, B. (2002). *The hip hop generation: Young blacks and the crisis in African American culture.* Basic Civitas Books.

Ladson-Billings, G. (1995). Toward a theory of culturally relevant pedagogy. *American Educational Research Journal, 32*(3), 465–491.

Ladson-Billings, G. (2006). From the achievement gap to the education debt: Understanding achievement in US schools. *Educational Researcher, 35*(7), 3–12.

Ladson-Billings, G. (2021). Three decades of culturally relevant, responsive, & sustaining pedagogy: What lies ahead? *The Educational Forum, 85*(4), 351–354.

Lamar, K. (2012). *Backseat freestyle. On good kid, m.A.A.d. city.* Top Dawg; Aftermath; Interscope.

Lorde, A. (1984). *Sister outsider: Essays and speeches.* Crossing Press.

Love, B. L. (2016). Complex personhood of hip hop & the sensibilities of the culture that fosters knowledge of self & self-determination. *Equity & Excellence in Education, 49*(4), 414–427.

Love, B. L. (2019). *We want to do more than survive: Abolitionist teaching and the pursuit of educational freedom.* Beacon Press.

Mirra, N., & Garcia, A. (2022). Guns, schools, and democracy: Adolescents imagining social futures through speculative civic literacies. *American Educational Research Journal, 59*(2), 345–380.

Patton, D. U., Eschmann, R. D., & Butler, D. A. (2013). Internet banging: New trends in social media, gang violence, masculinity and hip hop. *Computers in Human Behavior, 29*(5), A54–A59.

Richardson, E. (2006). *Hiphop literacies.* Routledge.

Rose, T. (2003). *Longing to tell: Black women talk about sexuality and intimacy*. Farrar, Straus and Giroux.

Rose, T. (2008). *The hip hop wars: What we talk about when we talk about Hip Hop – and why it matters*. Basic Civitas Books.

Scott, D. (2011, November 15). *Cover story uncut: Drake talks about romance, rap, and what's really real*. Complex. www.complex.com/music/2011/11/cover-story-uncut-drake-talks-romance-rap-really-real

Sealey-Ruiz, Y. (2013). Using urban youth culture to activate the racial literacy of Black and Latino male high school students. In A. Cohan & A. Honigsfeld (Eds.), *Breaking the mold of education: Innovative and successful practices for student engagement, empowerment, and motivation* (pp. 3–10). Rowman & Littlefield Education.

Seider, S., Graves, D., El-Amin, A., Kelly, L., Soutter, M., Clark, S., Jennett, P., & Tamerat, J. (2021). The development of critical consciousness in adolescents of color attending "opposing" schooling models. *Journal of Adolescent Research*. https://doi.org/10.1177/07435584211006466

Shor, I. (1999). What is critical literacy. *Journal for Pedagogy, Pluralism & Practice, 4*(1), 1–26.

Technique, I. (2001). Dance with the devil. In *On revolutionary Vol. 1*. Self Released.